MW00962931

PONTIFICAL COUNCIL FOR JUSTICE AND PEACE

FROM STOCKHOLM TO JOHANNESBURG

An Historical Overview of the Concern
of the Holy See for the Environment

1972-2002

Sister Marjorie Keenan, RSHM

VATICAN CITY 2002

ISBN 88-209-7352-9

VATICAN PRESS

TABLE OF CONTENTS

Presentation   9

Introductory Note   11

Chapter One. Leading to the Stockholm Conference   13

Part I   Reading the Signs of the Times   14
           Vatican Council II   14
           The Second Synod of Bishops   15

Part II   The Early Teaching of Pope Paul VI   16
           Encyclical and Apostolic Letters   16
           Major Addresses   17

Part III   Conclusion   18

Part IV   Overview form 1964 to 1972   19
           Theological and moral concepts   19
           Some practical consequences   19
           *Principles of the Social Teaching of the Church cast in a
           new light*   20
           *The intimate relationship between care for the environment and
           spirituality*   20

**Chapter Two. From Stockholm to the End of the Pontificate of Pope
           Paul VI: 1972-1978**   21

Part I   The Stockholm Conference   21
           A Papal Message   21
           The Holy See at the Stockholm Conference   22

Part II   Papal Teaching in the Post-Stockholm Period   23

Part III   Conclusion   24

Part IV   Overview from 1972 to 1978   25
           Creation as the common patrimony of all of humanity   25
           The global nature of the environmental problem   25
           The human person within creation   25
           Integral development and the environment   26
           Solidarity   26

Chapter Three. The Early Pontificate of Pope John Paul II: 1978 to 1989 27

Part I   Care for the Environment: A Question that Cannot be Ignored . . . 27

Part II   The Urgency of the Message 31
          The moral responsibility of the person for the environment . . 31
          The rural world 32
          Modern scientific and technological development 34

Part III Conclusion 36

Part IV   Overview from 1978 to 1989 37
          General concepts 37
          The role of the human person in creation 38
          The use of God's creation 38
          Development 38

Chapter Four. Leading to the Rio Conference: 1990 through June 1992 39

Part I   Care for All of Creation 39
          Peace with God, Peace with All of Creation 39
          Centesimus Annus 42

Part II   The Immediate Preparation for the Rio Conference 43

Part III The Holy See and the Rio Conference 45
          Centrality of the human person 46
          The population question 46
          Defense of the poor 48
          The environmental impact of war 48

Part IV   Conclusion 49

Part V   Overview from 1990 through June 1992 50
          General Considerations 50
          The environmental question: its overall nature and components 51
          Selected moral principles 51

Chapter Five. Expanding and Deepening the Vision: 1992 through 1999 53

Part I   The Environment: An All-Embracing Concern 53
          Encyclical Letters 53
          Apostolic Exhortations 54

Part II   The Post-Rio Period: the Centrality of the Human Person in Creation 57

Part III Specific Social Questions 59
         Food Production 59
         Water 60
         Chemical Hazards 61

Part IV A Relationship with Nature 62
         Nature as revealing God 62
         The language of nature 62

Part V   The Activity of the Holy See – Rio + Five 63

Part VI Conclusion 64

**Chapter Six. A New Millennium: Towards the Future – 2000 leading
into 2002** 66

Part I   The Celebration of the Jubilee of the Year 2000 66
         The earth as gift of God to all 66
         Apostolic Letters and the Papal Bull 67

Part II The Goods of Creation are for All: A Challenge for the Agricul-
         tural World 68

Part III On the Eve of the Johannesburg Conference 71
         *The Holy See's Paper to the IV Preparatory Committee Meeting
         for the World Summit for Sustainable Development* 71
         The Venice Declaration 72

Part IV In Guise of Conclusion 74

Annexes

         Text One   Dogmatic Constitution *Lumen Gentium* . . . 79
         Text Two   Pastoral Constitution *Gaudium et Spes* 80
         Text Three   Second Synod of Bishops *Justice in the World* 84
         Text Four   Encyclical *Populorum Progressio* 85
         Text Five   Apostolic Letter *Octogesima Adveniens* . . . 87
         Text Six   Message to the Stockholm Conference 89
         Text Seven   Encyclical *Redemptor Hominis* 92
         Text Eight   Encylical *Sollicitudo Rei Socialis* 96
         Text Nine   Encyclical *Dominum et Vivificantem* 101

Text Ten   Encyclical *Laborem Exercens* 102
Text Eleven   Apostolic Letter *Amici Dilecti* 106
Text Twelve   Address to the UN Centre, Nairobi, Kenya . . 108
Text Thirteen   1990 World Day of Peace Message 114
Text Fourteen   Encyclical *Centesimus Annus* 123
Text Fifteen   Encyclical *Evangelium Vitae* 127
Text Sixteen   Encyclical *Fides et Ratio* 129
Text Seventeen   Apostolic Exhortation *Vita Consecrata* 130
Text Eighteen   Apostolic Exhortation *Ecclesia in America* . . 131
Text Nineteen   Apostolic Exhortation *Ecclesia in Asia* 132
Text Twenty   Apostolic Exhortation *Ecclesia in Oceania* . . 133
Text Twenty-One   Apostolic Letter *Tertio Millennio Adveniente* 134
Text Twenty-Two   Bull of Indiction *Incarnationis Mysterium* . . 136

Appendices

Appendix One   The Holy See's Paper to the IV Preparatory
                      Committee Meeting for the World Summit for
                      Sustainable Development 141

Appendix Two   The Venice Declaration 149

PRESENTATION

In a world of rapid change, it is good to stop at times in order to look back, not to look back to see the path followed but rather to discover the wealth of that past which so often we did not have time to savor in our haste to move on. The United Nations World Summit for Sustainable Development offers us an opportunity to do so. It is taking place just thirty years after the United Nations Conference on the Human Environment that awakened so many to the seriousness of the environmental degradation.

Within the Social Teaching of the Catholic Church, the environmental question is often considered of only recent concern. Yet, if we look back to the time of the Second Vatican Council, we can discover in its documents the solid roots of a formal and informal teaching concerning care for the environment that has consistently grown over the years. From the Dogmatic Constitution *Lumen Gentium* of November 1964 to the Venice Declaration of June 2002, the message has been the same: we have a moral obligation to care for the environment, to respect all of God's creation and to assure that its goods are equitably shared with all.

This book intends to help us to reflect on this responsibility. Yet, its scope is limited. It simply presents an overview of the teaching of Pope Paul VI and of Pope John Paul II concerning care for the environment. It begins with a consideration of the Second Vatican Council, the teaching of which lay a solid foundation for this reflection. Then for each subsequent time period, the rich teaching of papal Encyclicals and Apostolic Exhortations is presented and the texts referred to given in annex.

The participation of the Holy See in the UN Conferences from Stockholm to Johannesburg is also traced. The questions that the Holy See addresses during such Conferences are more specific and specifically related to the agenda of the Conference. Finally, both Pope Paul VI and Pope John Paul II have spoken on the environment to various groups and on a wide variety of occasions. Because of the abundance of material, a choice had to be made and only certain topics of particular relevance today are included in the overview.

The book is therefore an invitation to go further and, above all, to reflect carefully on the teachings of the Catholic Church concerning the environment. These teachings call for radical change: for a conversion of the heart and mind so that all may have life, life in abundance. This implies living in harmony with all of creation. When this is so, the world will truly be at peace and all of creation will reflect the beauty of the Creator.

29 June 2002

✠ GIAMPAOLO CREPALDI

Titular Bishop of Bisarcio
Secretary of the Pontifical Council
for Justice and Peace

INTRODUCTORY NOTE

From the time of Vatican Council II, Popes Paul VI and John Paul II have spoken with extraordinary frequency of the moral obligation to care for the environment. The following pages present the broad outlines of this teaching. The approach adopted is that of an historical overview that respects a certain chronology. There is therefore no pretence of analyzing this rich material. Given the extraordinary number of texts available, those referred are necessarily limited.

Pride of place is therefore given to the more formal papal magisterium: that of Encyclicals, Apostolic Exhortations and Apostolic Letters. The pertinent sections of these documents can be found in the Annex. The references to Scripture are those commonly used. The list of abbreviations adopted to refer to papal documents is given. For papal addresses or messages, the translation is that of the weekly English Edition of *L'Osservatore Romano*.

ABBREVIATIONS

AD	Apostolic Letter *Amici Dilecti*
CA	Encyclical Letter *Centesimus Annus*
DV	Encyclical Letter *Dominum et Vivificantem*
E in A	Apostolic Exhortation *Ecclesia in Asia*
EA	Apostolic Exhortation *Ecclesia in America*
EO	*Apostolic Exhortation Ecclesia in Oceania*
EV	Encyclical Letter *Evangelium Vitae*
FR	Encyclical Letter *Fides et Ratio*
GS	Pastoral Constitution *Gaudium et Spes*
IM	Bull of Indiction *Incarnationis Mysterium*
JW	Synodal Document *Justice in the World*
LE	Encyclical Letter *Laborem Exercens*
LG	Dogmatic Constitution *Lumen Gentium*
NMI	Apostolic Letter *Novo Millennio Ineunte*
OA	Apostolic Letter *Octogesima Adveniens*
PP	Encyclical Letter *Populorum Progressio*
RH	Encyclical Letter *Redemptor Hominis*
SRS	Encyclical Letter *Sollicitudo Rei Socialis*
TMA	Apostolic Letter *Tertio Millennio Adveniente*
VC	Apostolic Exhortation *Vita Consecrata*
WDP	World Day of Peace Message

Chapter One

LEADING TO THE STOCKHOLM CONFERENCE

While this historical overview traces the development of papal teaching concerning care for the environment from the time of the 1972 Stockholm Conference on the Human Environment to the present, it begins with a brief consideration of certain highly significant texts of the Second Vatican Council. These actually establish a basis for the consideration of a then emerging problem that is directly related to the longstanding teaching of the Church on creation and the place of the human person within it.

Part I examines the texts not only of the Second Vatican Council but also of the Second Synod of Bishops dedicated to justice in the world. Part II briefly considers the relevant teachings of Pope Paul VI prior to the Stockholm Conference, while Part III presents the salient moral and theological concepts of this initial period.

At the time of the 1972 United Nations Conference on the Human Environment, held in Stockholm, a growing number of people had become keenly aware of the increasing degradation of the natural environment throughout the world. The new and highly diversified ecological movements of that period not only did not turn to or include the Catholic Church but occasionally proposed solutions to environmental problems that were contrary to its teaching. Yet, at the very same time, the moral obligation to care for the environment found a strong and fresh echo within a Church that had been newly challenged by the Second Vatican Council to read the signs of the times.[1]

---

[1] Pastoral Constitution *Gaudium et Spes*, 7 December 1965, No. 11.

13

Part I

Reading the Signs of the Times

Vatican Council II

With startling clarity, the Dogmatic Constitution *Lumen Gentium*[2] made reference to a series of biblical texts concerning the redemption not only of the human person but also of all creation.[3] It also clearly stated the value of all of creation in its own right.[4] The human person was, moreover, to order creation to the praise of God through work that would contribute to the bettering not only of society but also of the whole of creation.[5] While the goods of the earth were to be used rationally, there was also an urgent need to assure their better distribution.[6]

The Pastoral Constitution *Gaudium et Spes*[7] also stressed that created things had their own laws and values, adding that the human person must learn them. *All* persons bear the heavy responsibility of completing the work of creation. Believers, no matter what their religion, have moreover " always recognized the voice and the revelation of God in the language of creatures ".[8] Following the thought of *Lumen Gentium, Gaudium et Spes* reiterated that God had destined the goods of the earth for all, and that they must be distributed in a way " regulated by justice and accompanied by charity ".[9] But care for the earth goes still further. The human person can, and indeed must, love the goods of God's creation. " It is as flowing from God's hand that he looks upon them and reveres them " and uses them in a spirit of poverty and freedom.[10]

---

[2] Dogmatic Constitution *Lumen Gentium,* 21 November 1964, Nos. 36, 41, 48. [Text One]

[3] *LG* No. 48: *Acts* 3: 21; *Eph* 1: 10; *Col* 1: 20; *2 Pt* 3: 10-13. Cf. also *LG* No. 36: *Rm* 8: 21; *1 Cor* 15: 27-28.

[4] *LG* No. 36.

[5] *LG* No. 41.

[6] *LG* No. 36.

[7] *GS* Nos. 34, 36, 37, 57, 69. [Text Two] The Decree *Apostolicam Actuositatem* No. 7 takes up the same themes noting in addition that created goods receive added dignity in their relationship to the human person.

[8] Cf. *GS* No. 36 as well as *GS* No. 34 and 69.

[9] *GS* No. 69.

[10] *GS* No. 37, 3. These references and those of other texts indicated above show how

These short but highly significant references in major conciliar documents constituted a solid theological framework for the Church as it started more consciously and consistently to address the growing environmental crisis.

The Second Synod of Bishops

After the Second Vatican Council, Pope Paul VI began to convoke Synods, that is meetings of bishops from across the world, to discuss very specific topics. Lay advisors and special assistants also attend. In 1971, he held a second Post-Conciliar Synod to address the question of *Justice in the World*.[11] Its final document carried still further the thought of the Church concerning care for the environment, noting that people were beginning "to grasp a new and more radical dimension of unity", that of their shared environment.[12] The resources of the earth – as well as air and water – are not infinite but rather must be conserved as a unique patrimony of all humanity.[13] The problems of the richer nations – whether capitalist or socialist – make such demands on resources and energy supplies that irreparable damage would be done if their high rates of consumption and pollution were extended to the whole of humanity.[14]

Those who are already rich are bound to accept a different lifestyle in order to avoid destroying a heritage that they are "obliged by absolute justice" to share with all other members of the human race.[15] A new recognition of the material limits of the biosphere, of the unequal distribution of goods and of other modern phenomena proper to the highly developed part of the world had led to the awareness that "in today's world new modes of understanding human dignity are arising".[16] This last statement estab-

deeply this teaching is rooted in Scripture, the Fathers of the Church, and St. Thomas Aquinas. Reference is also made to texts of Pope Pius XII and Pope John XXIII.

[11] *Justice in the World*, Final Document of the Second Synod of Bishops, 30 November 1971. Since there are no paragraph numbers in the text, reference is made to the Chapter and number of the paragraph within that Chapter. [Text Three]

[12] *Ibid.* Ch. I, Para. 2.

[13] *Ibid.*

[14] *Ibid.* Ch. I, Para. 5.

[15] *Ibid.* Ch. III, International Action, Proposition No. 7.

[16] *Ibid.* Ch. I, Para 6.

lishes a significant link between human dignity, care for the environment, and sustainable development. This relationship remains key in the Church's approach to the environmental question.

Part II

The Early Teaching of Pope Paul VI

Encyclicals and Apostolic Letters

While direct references to the environment are limited in *Populorum Progressio*,[17] their context is highly significant: that of the development of peoples. The Encyclical addresses the key question of the role of human persons in creation. They were given the responsibility, through their intelligence and work, "to complete and perfect it" by their own efforts and to their own advantage.[18] Great importance is also given to the closely related question of the right of all peoples to the goods of this earth.[19]

The tone of *Octogesima Adveniens*[20] is decidedly more urgent. People were suddenly becoming aware of the dramatic consequences of an ill-considered exploitation of nature. Because of uncontrolled industrial development in the richer sections of the world, the environment was becoming a perpetual menace: pollution, refuse, new illnesses coupled with an immense destructive power. It could be legitimately asked whether "man is not turning back against himself the results of his conquests".[21] Having tried to control nature, is he not becoming the slave of

[17] Encyclical Letter *Populorum Progressio,* 26 March 1967, Nos. 22, 25, 27, 28. [Text Four] Cf. also No. 23.

[18] *Ibid.* No. 22.

[19] The language of *Populorum Progressio* concerning the environment does not seem to reflect fully that of the documents of Vatican II and of *Justice in the World* as regards the value of created goods in their own right. This could simply be due to the lack of an as yet organic development of a specific teaching on the environment, a relatively new concern for the Church.

[20] Apostolic Letter *Octogesima Adveniens,* 14 May 1971, Nos. 9, 21. [Text Five]

[21] *OA* No. 9.

16

the objects he produces?[22] In fact, people were suddenly becoming aware that by an ill-considered exploitation of nature, they risked destroying it. This awareness was not enough however; it had to be coupled with action. Together with all others, Christians must assume responsibility for a destiny that is now shared by all.[23]

Major Addresses

In his addresses to various groups before the Stockholm Conference, Pope Paul VI consistently returned to central points concerning the relationship of the human person to the environment, at the same time bringing out significant new aspects which both enrich and complete this teaching. Turning to the scriptural basis for a correct understanding of this relationship, he reminded States that if the Bible presents creation as the work of the Creator, it has been given over to the work of the creature who is to exploit it intelligently, humanizing it as it were, while enjoying its fruits as a gift of God.[24] Through their work, people perfect and transform all of creation. To do so according to Gods' plan, they must respect the earth. They must also admire, explore and know it.[25]

Still more, the human person is called to love the earth,[26] seeing in it the image of the Creator.[27] Nature actually speaks: "nothing is without a voice, without language".[28] Pope Paul VI refers to the *Hexameron* of St. Ambrose which "has beautiful pages on animal life, and the ways in which it manifests the wisdom and providence of the Creator".[29] He also speaks of meditating on what he calls "an incisive and paradoxical statement" of Teilhard de Chardin concerning "the spiritual power of matter".[30]

---

[22] *Ibid.*

[23] *Ibid.* No. 21.

[24] Address to the International Labor Organization, 10 June 1969.

[25] Address to the World Wildlife Fund, 21 June 1969.

[26] Address to Agricultural Workers, 22 April 1964.

[27] Address to the World Wildlife Fund, 21 June 1969.

[28] Address to the International Institute of Juridical Studies, 27 March 1971. [Original French]

[29] Address to the World Wildlife Fund, 21 June 1969.

[30] Address to the International Institute of Juridical Studies, 27 March 1971.

It was moreover clear that, to preserve the environment, a radical change of behavior had become urgent.[31] Not only must the human person learn "to dominate his domination" of the earth,[32] environmental law and regulation were becoming more necessary with every passing day.[33]

Part III

Conclusion

Within this relatively brief period, Paul VI had significantly deepened key concepts of the Social Teaching of the Church and with decided clarity applied them to one of the most serious problems of his time, one which the world continues to face today. His vision remains clear and strong, deeply rooted in Scripture and the principles of the Social Teaching of the Church. Yet he wrote at a time when the environment was still considered a marginal issue by the vast majority of people, above all in the developed countries. The question, however, remains so urgent that these same concepts will continue to be developed with a certain consistency to the present time.

It is evident that in the series of conciliar and papal texts considered, we find long-standing concepts of the Social Teaching of the Church that find fresh application in response to what was then the still emerging problem of the environment. Without any pretension of being complete, the salient principles and concepts of this important period can be outlined as follows.[34]

---

[31] Address to the Food and Agriculture Organization, 16 November 1970. Cf. No. 3-4.

[32] *Ibid.*

[33] Address to the International Institute of Juridical Studies, 27 March 1971.

[34] This same method will be followed throughout this study. This outline is, however, only indicative. A transversal analytical study would be necessary in order to refine them, but this is beyond the scope of this text.

Part IV

Overview from 1964 to 1972

1. *Theological and moral concepts*

   - All of creation has a value in its own right.

   - Created things have their own laws and values that the human person must learn.

   - There is a delicate balance in the natural milieu that must be respected.

   - An irrational exploitation of the natural resources can have serious consequences.

   - The human person is responsible for completing the work of creation in view of the betterment of society and also that of the whole of creation.

   - There is consequently an intimate relationship between care for the environment and sound development.

   - The goods of the earth are a unique patrimony of all of humanity.

   - Their distribution must be regulated by justice and accompanied by love.

2. *Some practical consequences*

   - When action is undertaken, it is important to consider the consequences of any intervention in the existing natural equilibrium.

   - The present high rate of consumption and pollution is not tolerable.

   - The richer nations must accept a different lifestyle in order to avoid destroying a heritage that they are obliged by justice to share with all members of the human race.

   - There is an urgent need for environmental law and regulation.

3. Principles of the Social Teaching of the Church cast in a new light

- There is a growing awareness that the preservation of the environment is a new and radical dimension of *unity*.

- New modes of understanding *human dignity* are also arising that take into account the state of the environment in which the person lives.

4. The intimate relationship between care for the environment and spirituality

- We must listen to the voice of nature; nothing is without a voice.

- Believers, no matter what their religion, "have always recognized the voice and the revelation of God in the language of creation" (*GS* No. 36).

- There is a need to admire nature, seeing in it the reflection of the Creator.

- The human person is to order all of creation to praise God.

Chapter Two

FROM STOCKHOLM TO THE END
OF THE PONTIFICATE OF POPE PAUL VI
1972-1978

This brief period is not without its particular significance. During it, Pope Paul VI addressed a major message to the Stockholm Conference on Human Development that outlined the teaching of the Holy See on a question of increasing concern. He affirmed that a sound environment and the possibility of the integral development of all peoples were closely connected. They must ultimately be taken as a whole.

After considering the overall contribution of the Holy See to the Stockholm Conference in Part I, a brief review is made of the ongoing action of the Holy See in the follow-up period. Pope Paul VI spoke several times on the question and representatives of the Holy See continued to attend all major United Nations meetings dedicated to the environment.

Part I

The Stockholm Conference

A Papal Message

The Message of Pope Paul VI to the Stockholm Conference on the Human Environment can rightly be considered a highly significant statement outlining the Church's concern for the environment.[1] Its approach to the environmental question is clearly global in intent; there is but one earth. Since the nature of the environmental problem is such that abuses in one part of the world have repercussions in others, it is clear that efforts to solve this problem similarly require the cooperation of all.

This Message gave a new and full expression to the concept of the integral development of the human person of *Populorum Progressio*. To

[1] Message to the UN Conference on Human Environment addressed to Mr. Maurice Strong, Secretary General of the Conference, 1 June 1972. [Text Six]

assure such a development, people must be set within their environment, because the environment conditions the life of those who are called to perfect and ennoble their milieu through their presence, work and contemplation. This is but one striking example of Paul VI's rich understanding of a certain mutuality in the relationship of the human person with the environment.

While generally positive in his approach to science and technology, Paul VI does not hesitate to point out the ambivalence of their indiscriminate use. The industrialization process must also be examined. The growing pollution from industry affects not only the health of the human person but also the well-being of animals and plants as well.

In the thought of Paul VI, human solidarity clearly extends into the future. The obligation to care for the earth includes that of assuring that future generations will inherit an earth that is habitable. For this to be realized, material growth must be controlled. This requires a change in lifestyle and a moderation in the use of food resources. The human person is, in fact, called to transform the world into a beautiful abode where everything is respected.

The Holy See at the Stockholm Conference

The contribution of the Holy See to the Stockholm Conference was not limited to the Message of Pope Paul VI. The Head of the Delegation of the Holy See also addressed the Conference, indicating the precise points on which the Holy See felt able to make a specific contribution.

- In a technological civilization, it is only when the human person determines *to be more* rather than *to have more* that harmony between man and nature will be restored.

- If care for the environment is set within the context of real development, adequate policies will be more easily determined on both a national and international level.

- The developing countries must set for themselves their model of civilization.

• The State of Vatican City is concerned for the environment on its own territory as well as on that which is under its jurisdiction and which holds a unique cultural and artistic patrimony.[2]

The following year, the Pontifical Commission for Justice and Peace[3] published a study by the noted English economist Dr. Barbara Ward entitled *A New Creation? Reflections on the Environmental Issue.*[4] While this was a groundbreaking publication for the Pontifical Commission for Justice and Peace, the environmental question does not seem to have been central to its regular program of work in this initial period of its existence.

Part II

Papal Teaching in the Post-Stockholm Period

In the brief period between the end of the Stockholm Conference and the death of Pope Paul VI, no Encyclicals or Apostolic Letters mentioned the environmental question. However, Paul VI made a significant address to the Pontifical Academy of Sciences during a Study Week on Biological and Artificial Membranes.[5] The precise topic of the meeting was the desalination of water.

His immediate concern was the relationship between the lack of reserves of fresh water and the hindering of development, that is the relationship between the activity of the human person and the good of all of humanity, including that of future generations. It is interesting to note that he considered solidarity with future generations as a form of love to which many were sensitive, especially in regard to care for the environment. He also stressed that human intelligence must discover the secret possibilities of nature and apply them to a development that is according to God's plan.

---

[2] Statement of the Holy See, 7 June 1972.

[3] In June 1988, the name of this Dicastery of the Roman Curia, founded in 1967, was changed to the Pontifical Council for Justice and Peace. This title will generally be used throughout the text.

[4] This was the fifth in a series of brochures published by the Pontifical Commission as a follow-up to the 1971 Synod of Bishops, but it falls within the context of the Stockholm Conference.

[5] 19 April 1975.

Yet a note of caution had already been sounded. While man's desire for knowledge can make him accede to a new relationship with nature, it cannot be forgotten that he is also capable of destroying his surroundings.[6]

Throughout this period, increasing emphasis was put on the need for the developed nations to adopt a lifestyle that would exclude both an excessive consumption and a production aimed at meeting superfluous needs. The present lifestyle not only had a negative effect on nature but also on the moral fiber of the human person.[7] There continued to be a repeated call to both a simplicity of lifestyle and to a sense of universal solidarity. It must never be forgotten that creation is a common patrimony of all of humanity.[8] This is perhaps at the heart of the Church's concern for the environment. It is impossible to separate care for creation and the good of all.

The representatives of the Holy See also regularly spoke on environment-related issues during various United Nations meetings and conferences. As early as 1970, the President of the Pontifical Commission for Justice and Peace, Cardinal Maurice Roy, had sent a message to the Secretary General of the United Nations on the occasion of the launching of the Second Development Decade. He spoke of the need to undertake a fundamental reconsideration of the planet's resource use and management so "that the increasingly irrational levels of extravagance, waste and pollution of the 'high consumption societies' should not jeopardize the poor nations' hopes of development and humanity's ultimate hopes of survival".[9]

Part III

Conclusion

During this period, both Pope Paul VI and the representatives of the Holy See had consistently stressed the importance of care for the environment. It would seem clear, however, that many of the members of the Church remained unaware of this. The link between their religious belief

---

[6] Letter to the Director General of UNESCO on the occasion of the Eighth World Day of Alphabetization; 7 September 1974.

[7] UN Special Session on Raw Materials and Development, 4 March 1975.

[8] Message for the Fifth World Environment Day, 7 June 1977.

[9] 19 November 1970.

and their obligation to care for God's creation was not explicitly drawn out in systematic educational and catechetical programs. Another factor that hindered this integration of belief and action could have been the radicality of certain ecological movements that actually resulted in their appearing to be marginal.

As for the earlier period, certain concepts seemed to dominate. In addition to those already identified, others were cast in a new light. As before, they are simply outlined below.

Part IV

Overview from 1972 to 1978

1. *Creation as the common patrimony of all of humanity*

   - The patrimony of humanity extends to the sea and to outer space, the benefits of which must be for all.
   - This places limits on all resource use and management.
   - This patrimony must be passed on to future generations; their world must be habitable.

2. *The global nature of the environmental problem*

   - Environment damage often knows no frontiers. Consideration must therefore be given to the possible repercussions of abuse in one part of the world on other regions.
   - This particular nature of the problem requires the cooperation of all in seeking adequate solutions.

3. *The human person within creation*

   - Human persons are to live in harmony with their environment.
   - The human intelligence must discover the secrets of nature.
   - Human persons are called to care for and develop their environment by their presence, work and contemplation.

4. *Integral development and the environment*

- True development cannot take place when the environment within which a person lives is abused.

- Science and technology have contributed much to progress. However, there are moral limits to their use and applications, among which their effect on the environment.

- The environmental impact of the industrialization process must also be taken into consideration and corrected when necessary.

5. *Solidarity*

- Solidarity is universal. It extends to all, including to future generations.

- These two aspects of solidarity condition the approach to care for the environment.

Chapter Three

THE EARLY PONTIFICATE OF POPE JOHN PAUL II
1978 to 1989

The contribution of Pope John Paul II to the moral obligation to promote a sound environment for all is both comprehensive and highly differentiated. Taken as a whole, it forms an articulated body of most relevant material, the richness of which still remains to be fully explored and even more importantly applied. Because of its extent, its presentation is divided into three periods.

The first period extends from 1978 through 1989 and is the focus of the present chapter. The growing concern for the environment is mirrored in the attention that Pope John Paul II gives to the question in several major documents dating from this period. Part I briefly summarizes their content, while Part II traces the sense of urgency that John Paul II increasingly conveys. A brief consideration of selected topics makes this clear. An overview of some of the dominant concepts dealt with in this period closes the chapter.

Part I

Care for the Environment:
A Question that Cannot be Ignored

Pope John Paul II's first Encyclical *Redemptor Hominis*[1] is generally considered programmatic. It is significant, therefore, that care for the environment is one of the first social questions that he addresses. He does so with a certain originality that brings out clearly the relationship between religious belief and behavior. *Redemptor Hominis* carefully relates the fundamental doctrines of creation and redemption to present-day environmental problems. A case in point is that the creation that God saw as " very

---

[1] Encyclical Letter *Redemptor Hominis,* 4 March 1979. Cf. Nos. 8, 15, 16 *passim.*
[Text Seven]

good "[2] had been "subjected to futility"[3] through sin, and is still waiting to be set free.[4] What are the signs of this subjugation of the earth today? The first among the troubling phenomena that John Paul II cites is "the threat of pollution of the natural environment in areas of rapid industrialization".[5] The world of new and extraordinary conquests in the field of science and technology is also a sign that the world is still "groaning in travail".[6]

Modern men and women are, moreover, afraid and even seem threatened by much of what they produce and fear that it can radically turn against them.[7] This is due in part to their alienation from nature, which they exploit not only for industrial but also for military purposes as well as for uncontrolled technological development. They seem to see in the natural environment no other meaning than what serves for their immediate use and consumption. It is the Creator's will that the human person should communicate with nature as an intelligent "master" and "guardian", not as an "exploiter" and "destroyer".[8] This raises several serious questions about the ultimate outcome of present trends. There is a fundamental need "for solicitude by man for man, for his humanity, and for the future of people on earth".[9]

The Encyclical *Sollicitudo Rei Socialis*,[10] written on the occasion of the twentieth anniversary of Paul VI's *Populorum Progressio,* continues to convey the same sense of urgency about the need to care for the environment if the peoples of the earth are to enjoy true development. Among the positive signs in today's world is, in fact, a greater realization of the limits of available resources, of the need to respect the

[2] *Gn* 1: 31.
[3] *Rm* 8: 20.
[4] *Rm* 8: 19-23 *passim.*
[5] *RH* No. 8. The other phenomena he mentions are: the continual armed conflicts that were breaking out, the perspective of self-destruction through the use of weapons of mass destruction and the lack of respect of the life of the unborn. These four issues have remained central to the thought of John Paul II throughout his pontificate.
[6] *Rm* 8: 22.
[7] *RH* No. 15.
[8] *RH* No. 8, No. 15 *passim.*
[9] *RH* No. 15.
[10] Encyclical Letter *Sollicitudo Rei Socialis,* 30 December 1987, Nos. 26, 29, 30, 34.
[Text Eight]

integrity and the cycles of nature and to take them into account in development planning.[11]

Development must include respect for the order inherent to the natural world or cosmos.[12] Several considerations flow directly from this. The first is that one cannot use with impunity the different categories of beings – animals, plants, the natural elements. On the contrary, one must consider the nature of each being and its mutual connection in an ordered system. The second is a still more urgent concern. Natural resources are limited; some are non-renewable. Using them as if they were inexhaustible puts their future availability at risk. In the same way, development and industrialization must respect both the limits on the use of the natural world and the impact of development on the environment.[13] In summary, when man refuses to submit to the rule of God, nature rebels against him and "no longer recognizes him as its 'master'".[14]

The previous year, John Paul II had issued an Encyclical on the Holy Spirit, *Dominum et Vivificantem*,[15] in which he spoke of the Incarnation as having a cosmic dimension. Christ united himself "in some way with the entire reality of man, which is also 'flesh' – and in this reality with all 'flesh', with the whole of creation".[16] Once again, he does not hesitate to go far beyond material considerations in exploring the relationship of the human person and creation. He states that the Incarnation signifies the taking up into unity with God not only human nature but "in a sense ... everything that is 'flesh': the whole of humanity, the entire visible and material world".[17] The Incarnation then also has a cosmic significance, a cosmic dimension.

In this light, everything that the human person does assumes its own particular importance. This is especially true of work. In fact, John Paul II considers a correct understanding of work as essential to a proper relationship of the human person to the rest of creation. He develops this

[11] *SRS* No. 26.
[12] *SRS* No. 34.
[13] *SRS* No. 34. Cf. also No. 29.
[14] *SRS* No. 30.
[15] Encyclical Letter *Dominum et Vivificantem*, 18 May 1986, No. 50. [Text Nine]
[16] *Ibid.*
[17] *Ibid.*

concept in his Encyclical *Laborem Exercens*.[18] If all are called to subdue the earth, work is part of the human person's very existence. Through work, human beings reflect the action of the Creator of the universe,[19] and the "subduing" of the earth becomes a participation in God's activity.[20]

Work is for the sole good neither of the individual nor of the family alone; it must be directed toward the good of society. For this to be, the human person must learn the deepest meaning and value of all creation.[21] Were this respectful approach to the use and transformation of the earth's resources dominant, the relationship between the human person and the earth from which all persons draw their sustenance would clearly be one of far greater harmony and equilibrium.

There is often a contemplative approach to nature in the writings of Pope John Paul II. He repeats again and again that nature both reflects and reveals the Creator who created all things good. In his Apostolic Letter *Amici Dilecti*,[22] John Paul II brings out the importance for youth not only of book knowledge but of actual contact with the visible world, with nature in order to learn the mystery of creation: its richness and variety. Visible beings are, in fact, an invitation to see the invisible through the "transparence of the world".[23] Youth must learn to read the book of nature. Today, the human person is the exploiter of nature. Yet nature was given for admiration and contemplation. It is a mirror reflecting the covenant of all of creation, centered in the human person, with the Creator.[24]

[18] Encyclical Letter *Laborem Exercens*, 14 September 1981. Cf. Nos. 4, 25. [Text Ten]

[19] *LE* No. 4.

[20] *LE* No. 25.

[21] *LE* No. 25, quoting *LG* No. 36.

[22] Apostolic Letter to Youth for the International Youth Year, *Amici Dilecti*, 31 March 1985, No. 14. [Text Eleven]

[23] *AD Ibid.*

[24] *AD Ibid.*

Part II

The Urgency of the Message

The moral responsibility of the person for the environment

In all of his teachings on the environment, John Paul II presupposes a clear understanding of the nature of creation. What then in God's plan is the hidden meaning of this world? First of all, God does not will evil nor disorder nor the destruction of nature. "He created *the world* to be habitable, *to be good*, beautiful, harmonious".[25] God is Love and the world bears a reflection of this creative love. "The refrain that runs throughout the story of the creation of the stars, the earth, the planets, the animals, and mankind is ' and God saw that all this was good, very good' ".[26]

During his visit to Kenya in August 1985, Pope John Paul II visited the United Nations Centre in Nairobi, home to the United Nations Environment Program. His major address on that occasion builds on this understanding.[27] He affirms that care for the environment is a serious question for the Church because it is linked to God's command to have dominion over all things. The very dignity of the human person requires that this responsibility be exercised in a way that truly serves the human family. Not only immediate needs but also those of future generations must be taken into account in using the resources of the earth. "All created goods are directed to the good of all humanity ".[28] Science and technology as well as material and economic development cannot be the ultimate determining factor. It is the human person, and especially communities and nations, *freely choosing* to face the problems *together*[29] that will determine the future. Nowhere can it be seen more clearly that the world is interdependent than as regards the environment.

Pope John Paul II again returns to the importance of human dignity, of the participation of the person in development projects. He notes that a concrete sign of a coordinated approach to care for the environment would

[25] Address to Youth of Europe, 8 October 1988, Strasbourg, France. No. I, B), 1-6.
[26] *Ibid.* No. I, B), 1.
[27] Address at the UN Centre, 18 August 1985, Nairobi, Kenya. [Text Twelve]
[28] *Ibid.* No. 2.
[29] Emphasis added.

be the transfer of appropriate technology coupled with the training of local people in the use of it. Local experts have bonds with their own people that give them a special sensitivity to local values and needs.[30]

This emphasis on the local level does not lessen the importance of a global approach to the environment but rather refines the conditions under which it should take place. Given the very nature of the environmental crisis, a global ethical perspective is indispensable. "The environment is not only the setting in which the great drama of human history is played out, but in a sense it is also an active participant in that drama ".[31] Any attempt, therefore, that ignores the solidarity that binds the human person to the environment or the necessity of a universal concern for the needs of all peoples will inevitably lead to further imbalances.[32]

Humanity is therefore faced with what is essentially a moral problem. Development cannot take place independently of the relationship of persons to the natural environment. Only human persons acting together can determine the quality of the relationship with their surrounding on which they are ultimately dependent for all that they need to sustain life itself.

Respect for nature actually favors peace.[33] In anticipation of his 1990 World Day of Peace Message, Pope John Paul II states that peace can only be achieved when human beings are reconciled with each other and with their natural universe.[34] Both peace and care for the environment are questions that embrace all aspects of life including that of our relationship with God.

The rural world

While the industrialization process has had serious environmental consequences, the agricultural sector is perhaps the first concerned by the state of the land. If the land itself is the gift of the Creator, the work of the human person makes it productive and capable of sustaining life, also a

[30] *Ibid.* No. 5.

[31] Address to the Participants in a Symposium organized by *Nova Spes*, 14 December 1989, No. 1.

[32] *Ibid.* No. 3.

[33] Address for World Environment Day, 4 June 1986. Cf. Homily at Punta Arenas, Chile, 4 April 1987, No. 7.

[34] 1979 World Day of Peace Message, Part II, 1.

gift of God.[35] As in all other cases, this gift must be used for the good of all and not to the advantage of the few.[36]

To care for the land as gift is to recognize that God's presence permeates the whole of created reality. " In a sense, the Creator ' *hides himself* ' in [the] life-giving process of nature. It is the human person...who is called to ' discover ' and ' unveil ' the presence of God and his action in all of creation ".[37] Those who work the land are therefore cooperating with the Creator in sustaining and nurturing life.[38]

Three attitudes should characterize those who work in the agricultural sector in their efforts to render the land fruitful. The first is gratitude to God for rain, sunshine and all that makes the land fruitful without the work of human hands. The second is one of care for the land so that it will produce for future generations. Farming is much more than a profit-making enterprise. The third is generosity in seeing that the fruits of the land are for all by freely sharing with others the knowledge gained concerning care for the earth and by promoting rural development across the world.[39] The virtue of solidarity also takes on a particular tonality in the rural world. " It grounds and nourishes *that peaceful and harmonious relationship of human beings with one another and with the cosmos*, which has been the fertile tradition of rural civilization ".[40]

Indigenous peoples generally live in a close relationship with their land that is based on their spiritual view of creation. This often leads them to live with the Creator in an attitude of trust, seeing the beauty of the land as coming from God's hands and therefore deserving of care and conservation.[41] They consequently respect the natural resources of the land and use them with care. In recent times, the encounter of their traditional cultures with dominant cultural patterns has often disrupted this way of life.

---

[35] Homily at Living History Farm, Des Moines, Iowa, USA, 4 October 1979, No. 1.

[36] Homily at Mass in Salvador da Bahia, 7 July 1980, No. 4. Cf. Address to Farmers and Workers, Legazpi City, Philippines, 21 February 1981, No. 3 and Homily for Agricultural Workers, Monterey, California, 17 September 1987, No. 4.

[37] Homily for Agricultural Workers, Monterey, No. 3.

[38] Homily at Living History Farm, No. 1. Cf. Homily at Mass in Salvador da Bahia, No. 4.

[39] Homily at Living History Farm, No. 2.

[40] Address to Farmers and Craftsmen at Martina Franca, Italy, 29 October 1989, No. 3.

[41] Homily during Mass for the Indigenous Peoples of Canada, 20 September 1987, No. 2, No. 5. Cf. also Address to the Indigenous Peoples, 20 September 1987, No. 6.

It is important that the indigenous peoples keep alive their cultures, including their care of the earth. This actually benefits the entire human family.[42]

Pope John Paul II makes an unexpected link between those who work the land and miners who work in the depths of the earth. Both have an element in common: their direct contract with the reality of nature. This enables them to discover its admirably ordered totality of mineral, vegetable and animal. They can see the vestiges of Divine Wisdom in it and go from the good things that are seen to the maker, "for from the greatness and beauty of created things comes a corresponding perception of their Creator" (cf. *Wis* 15: 15).[43]

Modern scientific and technological development

Modern society is also marked by rapidly increasing progress in the fields of science and technology that has made significant contributions to the good of human persons and to their overall quality of life. We now have the possibility of determining the future for good or for bad, but, paradoxically, this very power is the cause of increasing fragility. While the "dreams of centuries" have now been made possible, the same rapid developments in various fields also could make the world uninhabitable, the sea useless, the air dangerous and the sky fearful. As never before, ethics must take priority over science, an ethics that takes into consideration all zones of the planet.[44]

Likewise a technology that aims only at profit has not always been respectful of the environment. It suffices to consider climate change, the reduction of the ozone layer, deforestation, desertification and the growing problem of various forms of toxic waste. These phenomena can ultimately only be corrected through education to a new and respectful attitude towards the environment that includes a rational use of the resources of the earth. Such an effort must be worldwide given the global nature of environmental problems.[45]

[42] Address to American Native Peoples, 14 September 1987, 4.

[43] Address to Workers assembled at the Gran Sasso Tunnel, Italy, 30 August 1980, No. 3.

[44] Address to Young People of Romagna, Italy, 11 May 1986, No. 4-5.

[45] Pontifical Academy of Sciences, Address to Study Group on Environment, 6 November 1987, No. 1.

One of the most promising fields of scientific research, opening immense possibilities for the good of all is that of space exploration. The presence of the human person and of various objects and instruments in space has, however, raised a new question. To whom does space belong? John Paul II does not hesitate; the answer is clear. It belongs to the whole of humanity; it is something for the benefit of all.[46]

Space technology allows for observations that go far beyond anything that can be done by systems working on the surface of the earth. Through the use of satellites, exact data can be obtained concerning the condition of tracts of land, the flow of water as well as weather conditions that can be used, among other, to improve agriculture and to monitor the state of forests. This makes it possible to draw up programs that meet concrete situations, be they local or global.[47] These programs can help the world to overcome ecological disasters that have already been caused by human rapacity on earth, in the water and in the atmosphere. Harmony between the person and nature must be restored.[48]

Another urgent problem is a constant increase in the demand for energy that has led to a depletion of certain natural energy sources and to increasing deforestation. To meet this challenge not only must new energy sources be developed but governments must also attempt to develop a unified energy policy so that energy produced in one part of the world can be transferred to other regions. Serious efforts should be made to develop such natural energy sources, among which solar energy seems to offer rich possibilities. If certain other forms of energy could present potential dangers to humans or to the environment, these threats must be eliminated.[49] As with other goods, energy is to serve all, including future generations.[50]

[46] Pontifical Academy of Sciences, Address to Study Group on The Impact of Space Exploration on Mankind, 2 October 1984, No. 5.

[47] *Ibid.* No. 8.

[48] *Ibid.* No. 9.

[49] Cf. Address to Pontifical Academy of Sciences, 28 October 1986, No. 8 concerning specifically the dangers of nuclear energy.

[50] Pontifical Academy of Sciences, Study Week on Energy and Humanity, 14 November 1980.

Part III

Conclusion

Throughout the years 1978-1989, the thought of Pope John Paul II concerning the environment became increasingly specific. He repeatedly stressed that care for the environment is a moral obligation closely related to a person's relationship both to God and to the natural world. The promotion of a sound environment for all should therefore be a crucial factor in development programs.

Pope John Paul's eloquent words to a group of young people[51] go to the very heart of the profound mystery of the relationship between the Creator and creation, between the person and nature. In fact, he carefully links creation and resurrection with the concrete reality of the human person. The words speak for themselves and are, as it were, a summary of the overall thought of this period:

> The Resurrection of Jesus Christ is God's definite yes to his Son, to the Son of Man, God's definite yes to the whole of creation. In the transfiguration of the risen body of Christ begins the transfiguration of every creature, the "new creation" in which all creation will be transformed.
>
> Yes to life, yes to hope and the future. Yes to humanity, yes to creation and all nature... In the universal new consciousness of our concrete demands of Christian life we have a deeper, added motive to stand up with all people of good will for the preservation and protection of nature and of the environment as well as for natural values. For us, these are not only a valuable good in themselves, but they are also a gift entrusted by the Creator to loyal hands. All nature that surrounds us is a creation like us, creation with us, and shares a common destiny with us, in God himself, to find its ultimate destiny and fulfillment as the new heaven and the new earth. This certitude based on our faith is for us an even greater stimulus to a responsibly

[51] Address to Flemish-speaking Youth, Diocese of Osnabrück, Germany, 31 March 1989.

aware, indeed to a reverent, attitude to creation: with inanimate nature, with plants and animals, and most of all with our fellow men and women, in whom we recognize and acknowledge God's image...

Live in the awareness of the new creation that has its beginning in Christ's resurrection; in solidarity with all people and creatures live out the vocation of all creation to eternal participation in Christ's resurrection and glory.

During this period, once again certain concepts take on a special importance. Those given below could and should be completed by taking into consideration the overall teaching of Pope John Paul II during this particularly rich period.

Part IV

Overview from 1978 to 1989

1. *General concepts*

- Nature is a mirror reflecting the covenant of all of creation, centered in the human person, with the Creator.

- The Incarnation signifies the taking up into unity with God the whole of humanity as well as the entire visible and material world.

- The redemptive act of Jesus extends to all of creation, all of which shares a common destiny.

- The resurrection began the transfiguration of every creature. In it all creation will be transformed.

- There is an ordered system within creation that must be respected.

- The nature of environmental problems is such that there is need for a unified moral vision regarding the environment and a global ethic to address it.

2. *The role of the person in creation*

- The human person lives in close interdependence with the environment.
- The concept of solidarity extends also to solidarity with nature.
- Through work, the human person reflects the action of God in the world.
- The human person must have a new and respectful attitude towards the environment. This requires a form of ecological education.
- All are responsible for the good of the environment.

3. *The use of God's creation*

- The natural environment must not serve solely for consumption.
- There are limits to available resources that must be respected.
- Science and technology cannot be the determining factors in development.

4. *Development*

- True development is intimately related to care for the environment.
- Environmental programs must take into account the particular situation in the different regions.
- The universal destination of created goods also includes the benefits of space exploration.

Chapter Four

LEADING TO THE RIO CONFERENCE
1990 through June 1992

This short period was one of intense activity on the part of the Holy See. In 1990, Pope John Paul II dedicated his annual World Day of Peace Message to peace and the environment. It remains the only major papal document totally on the environment, and its principles remain remarkably pertinent today. During this same period, a delegation of the Holy See was actively involved in the preparations for the 1992 United Nations Conference on the Environment and Development.[1] Across the world, concern for the environment had also grown on all levels. No longer could the question be considered marginal, and its urgency continued to be reflected in the thought of Pope John Paul II who continued to reflect on the moral aspects of the destruction of the environment.

Part I presents the 1990 World Day of Peace Message as the panoramic background for the interventions of the Holy See at the Rio Conference. A major social Encyclical *Centesimus Annus* was issued in 1991 and added an important new aspect to this overall picture: economic growth and care for the environment. Part II looks selectively at the addresses of Pope John Paul II leading up to the Rio Conference, while Part III examines the chief issues that concerned the Holy See within the context of the Conference itself.

Part I

Care for All of Creation

Peace with God, Peace with All of Creation

At the beginning of each year since 1968, the Pope has issued a World Day of Peace Message that presents an aspect of peace that is particularly

---

[1] The United Nations Conference on the Environment and Development [UNCED] was held in Rio de Janeiro from 3 to 14 June 1992. It is commonly known as the Earth Summit or the Rio Conference. This latter name will be used throughout the text.

relevant at that time.[2] This Message is addressed not only to members of the Catholic Church but to a broad audience, including international bodies, governments and non-governmental organizations. The 1990 Message *Peace with God, Peace with All of Creation* focused on a question that at first glance could seem only marginally related to peace. Yet the very title of this Message is revelatory. Peace is a question of harmony, which traditionally concerns a person's relations with God and with all others. Pope John Paul II does not hesitate, however, to extend the concept of harmony to all of creation, entrusted by God to all for the good of all. The Message makes this integrated approach clear in its opening phrase: "In our day, there is a growing awareness that world peace is threatened not only by the arms race, regional conflicts and continued injustices among peoples and nations, but also by a lack of due *respect for nature*".[3] Peace is, in fact, a whole.

Those very values that are fundamental to a peaceful society apply also to the promotion of a sound and healthy environment, hence the need for "carefully coordinated solutions based on a morally coherent world view".[4] Care for the environment is not an option. In the Christian perspective, it forms an integral part of our personal life and of life in society. Not to care for the environment is to ignore the Creator's plan for *all* of creation and results in an alienation of the human person.[5] The seriousness of this statement still remains to be fully appreciated.

The Message continues: the increasing devastation of the earth is now apparent to all. It is the result of a "callous disregard" for the requirements of the order and harmony that govern nature itself. [6] What is to be done? In the environmental field, the factors to be considered and the problems to be addressed are almost countless. Yet the heart of the crisis lies elsewhere. "We must go to the source of the problem and face in its

---

[2] The celebration of an annual World Day of Peace on January 1, the occasion for a major papal Message, was an initiative of Pope Paul VI that Pope John Paul II gladly continued.

[3] 1990 *WDP* No. 1. [Text Thirteen]

[4] *Ibid.* No. 2. Cf. also Address to the Ambassador of Papua New Guinea, 5 January 1991.

[5] *WDP* No. 3.

[6] *Ibid.* No. 5.

entirety that profound moral crisis *of which the destruction of the environment is only one troubling aspect*".[7]

It is against this strong moral background that the Message for the World Day of Peace turns to such questions as the proper use of science and technology so that the delicate balance of the ecosystems not be disturbed, the control of emissions that damage the ozone layer or result in climate modifications, as well as the need for a rational use of natural resources. Great caution must also be exercised as regards any form of genetic manipulation or the development of new forms of plant and animal life. In an area as delicate as this, indifference to ethical norms could lead humanity to the threshold of self-destruction.[8] There is an integrity to all of creation that cannot be ignored.

This mutual interdependence within creation also means that the few cannot destroy the environment or exhaust its resources for their own benefit while masses of people are living in misery. As said repeatedly from the time of Pope Paul VI, care for the environment and the integral development of all persons and societies are closely related. A new solidarity is now called for that must take into consideration not only the needs of all peoples but also the protection of the environment in view of the good of all. Such a determination would, moreover, lead to new opportunities for strengthening cooperative and peaceful relationships among States.[9]

Before such a panorama, it is clear that modern society must take a serious look at its lifestyle. A consumer society of instant gratification not only ultimately weakens the moral fiber of persons and societies but also leads to a type of social selfishness in which the needs of the other are ignored. Any education in ecological responsibility must therefore include education to responsibility for others as well as for the earth. Churches and religious bodies, non-governmental and governmental organizations all have a specific role to play in this education.[10]

The promotion of a sound and healthy environment and that of peace are also intimately linked. War and conflict cause not only an unacceptable

---

[7] *Ibid.*
[8] *Ibid.* No. 7.
[9] *Ibid.* No. 10.
[10] *Ibid.* No. 13.

loss of innocent lives but lead to incalculable damage to the environment: that is to land, crops, and water sources to mention only a few of its effects. The threat also still remains of the possible use of weapons that are capable of altering the balance of nature.[11]

Centesimus Annus

These same issues are taken up in the Encyclical *Centesimus Annus*.[12] The overall focus of the Encyclical is, however, on modern social and economic questions. Within this context also, serious consideration must be given to care for the environment. Pope John Paul II is quick to note that one of the specific problems and threats emerging in the advanced economies is that of a consumerism which is damaging to the environment. Because of a desire to have more and to enjoy rather than to be and to grow, persons are actually consuming the resources of the earth in an excessive and disordered way. At the root of this problem is an anthropological error.

> Man, who discovered his capacity to transform and in a certain sense create the world through his own work, forgets that it is always based on God's prior and original gift of the things that are… Instead of carrying out his role as a cooperator with God in the work of creation, man sets himself up in place of God and thus ends up provoking a rebellion on the part of nature, which is more tyrannized than governed by him.[13]

To meet the legitimate needs of those on the margins of society, Pope John Paul II again stresses that important changes may have to be made in established lifestyles in order to limit the waste of both natural and human resources so that all peoples of the earth may have a sufficient share of them.[14]

---

[11] *Ibid.* No. 11-12 *passim.*

[12] Encyclical Letter *Centesimus Annus*, 1 May 1991, Nos. 37, 38, 40, 50. [Text Fourteen] The Encyclical Letter *Redemptoris Missio* of 7 December 1990 had earlier included safeguarding the created world among the new problems facing the world, among which peace and development. Cf. No. 37.

[13] *CA* No. 37.

[14] *CA* No. 52.

Part II

The Immediate Preparation for the Rio Conference

In his 1990 World Day of Peace Message, John Paul II had called for a new solidarity. In his visit to Burkina Faso in January 1992, he gave a concrete example of this solidarity by making "*a solemn appeal to humanity* in the name of humanity itself".[15] The Pope had long been concerned with the peoples of the Sahel, affected by the harsh consequences of drought and desertification. In 1980, he had launched an appeal[16] that had resulted in the setting up in 1984 of the John Paul II Foundation for the Sahel to help those living in such harsh conditions to take their own responsibility for remedying the effects through the training of local personnel and the development of micro-projects in which local people could participate.

This new appeal was addressed to the peoples of the world, and especially to those of the North. What example were they giving to the rest of the world when the needs they created have now become necessities for themselves? Those of the North must become partners with the peoples of the Sahel, and while respecting their traditions and riches, help them to prevent their environment from becoming hostile and sterile.[17]

All must become aware of what is at stake if all are to collaborate in building a more livable world. This awareness will help people to be prepared for the necessary sacrifices in view of a reasonable balance between the demands of progress and the conservation of the natural patrimony. The challenge is double: helping people not only to live in solidarity with others but also to respect creation. Political authorities are in a position to help increase public awareness and to enact legislation that will help increase the necessary solidarity.[18] The problem is global, however, and its solution therefore also calls for "scientifically" based and internationally agreed standards.[19] Far from halting progress, the preservation of the envi-

---

[15] Appeal for the Sahel, Address at the headquarters of the Economic Community of Western Africa, Ouagadougou, Burkina Faso, 29 January 1990.

[16] Homily, Ouagadougou, Burkina Faso, 10 May 1980, No. 7 and No. 8.

[17] Cf. Appeal for the Sahel.

[18] Address to the Regional Council of Lazio, Italy, 5 February 1990.

[19] Address to the Ambassador of Korea to the Holy See, 30 March 1990.

ronment actually represents a challenge to creativity on the part of business leaders, who in turn also share in the responsibility for the promotion of a sound environment.[20]

An example of the complex consequences of destroying the delicate balance of nature is found in the large-scale destruction of tropical forests. Not only do these forests contribute to the regulation of the earth's climate, they are home to an immensely rich variety of species that are not only extraordinarily beautiful but also hold great potential for the production of medicines. These forests are threatened in many ways, including local needs for firewood, the demands of industry for hardwood, and inappropriate land use. If the human person is entitled to use the goods of creation, there are two basic moral limits that must be observed. The first is that no one may make use of nature against his or her own good or the good of others, including future generations. This directly concerns the choice of development models. The second is that the goods of the earth are entrusted to the human family. Their use therefore entails moral obligations. These two factors are actually be summed up by the very title of the 1990 World Day of Peace Message: *Peace with God the Creator, Peace with All of Creation.*[21]

Pope John Paul II has a profound sense of the integral harmony of the human person and the environment and therefore never hesitates to go from concrete considerations to the contemplation of creation. In one of his addresses to young people, he spoke of the different ways in which God communicates including through the springtime, the beauty of nature, "but he can also communicate himself through the purity of nature, through the winds, hurricanes and snow storms, everything that constitutes the dynamism of nature... All this can be God's self-communication; it can be a grace as well. He is also present because he is the Creator and the Creator is present in his creature, in every creature... This divine communication which comes about in all the wealth of creation is also an argument for ecology ".[22]

In this period leading up to the United Nations Conference on the Environment and Development, Pope John Paul II had continued to

<hr />

[20] Address to Business Leaders, Durango, Mexico, 9 May 1990, No. 8.

[21] Address to the Pontifical Academy of Sciences Study Week on Man and his Environment: Tropical Forests and the Conservation of Species, 18 May 1990.

[22] Address to Young People, Udine, Italy, 3 May 1992.

develop his broad and integrated approach to care for the environment, something that is intimately related not only to development and the choice of development models but also to peace in every part of the world. However, it is perhaps when he speaks directly of the relationship between the Creator and creation that it becomes most clear that the obligation to care for God's creation is all embracing, reaching down to the depths of each person, of all peoples.

On the eve of the Rio Conference, Pope John Paul II spoke of the aims of this important gathering. They reflect his thought over this short but significant period:

> This important meeting sets out to examine in depth the relationship between protection of the environment and the development of peoples. These are problems which have, at their roots, a profound ethical dimension, and which involve, therefore, the human person, the center of creation, with those rights of freedom which derive from his dignity of being made in the image of God and with the duties that every person has towards the future generations.[23]

Part III

The Holy See and the Rio Conference

Because of the extent of the environmental crisis and the Church's concern for the question, the Delegation of the Holy See was particularly active in the preparations for the United Nations Conference on the Environment and Development and participated fully in it with a high level delegation. While Pope John Paul II did not send a message to the Conference, Cardinal Angelo Sodano, Secretary of State, attended the high level segment of the Conference for Heads of State and Government.

What aspects of the environmental question did the representatives of the Holy See stress during the Conference? In this international forum, they explicitly drew on the vast magisterium of Popes Paul VI and John Paul II when addressing the ethical aspects of development and care for the environment.

---

[23] Address to Those Gathered in St. Peter's Square, 31 May 1992.

Centrality of the human person

The Holy See continued to insist on the centrality of the human person as regards both development and care for the environment. While all live in interdependence with the rest of creation, the human person is the only creature in the world " who is gifted with the intelligence to explore, the sagacity to utilize and is ultimately responsible for its choices and the consequences of those choices ".[24] All persons are therefore called to a solidarity of universal dimensions that embraces all of creation, entrusted to the care of all.

This basic principle gives rise to the related concepts of stewardship and solidarity. Stewardship extends to all of creation, while the universal destination of its goods includes not only natural resources but also those natural, spiritual, intellectual and technological goods necessary for the integral development of all persons and peoples.[25]

The population question[26]

Pope John Paul II had not directly addressed the relationship between population growth and environmental degradation before 1991. On 22 November of that year, he addressed the participants of a Study Week, under the sponsorship of the Pontifical Academy of Sciences, on accelerated increase in world population and the availability of natural resources. The principal concepts that are related to the Agenda of the Rio Conference were therefore presented in some detail.

---

[24] Archbishop Renato Martino, Intervention of the Holy See, 4 June 1992. Part I.

[25] The Holy See presented a Pro-memoria outlining its position concerning the main topics on the Agenda, cf. Bulletin of the Press Office of the Holy See No. 220/92, 30 May 1992. The interventions of Cardinal Angelo Sodano at high level segment of the Conference, 13 June 1992, and of Archbishop Martino on June 4, 1992 were also important elements in the contribution of the Holy See to the Conference.

[26] This topic had not been originally on the Agenda of the Conference. It began to become a point of contention in the preparatory process. The Director of the Holy See's Press Office therefore made a Declaration on the question on 25 May 1992 (Bulletin of the Press Office of the Holy See No. 208/92). The Pro-memoria stating the position of the Holy See regarding the matters dealt with by the Conference also addressed the population question in No. 9 and No. 10 (cf. Bulletin of the Press Office of the Holy See No. 220/92, 30 May 1992).

Pope John Paul II began his address to the Study Group by stating that the close connection between the world's resources and its inhabitants must be evaluated by taking into account the imbalances in demographic distribution, in movements of migrants and in the allocation and consumption of resources. The increase both of population and available resources varies widely from place to place. The scientific data that the Academy had been analyzing would help the Holy See in formulating "a carefully considered judgement of a religious and ethical nature". The data concerned not only the past but also future projections, particularly with regard to their impact on the environment.[27]

The resulting analysis pointed to a growing diversification concerning not only natural resources but also those actually capable of being used through the intelligence, enterprise and work of the human community, as for instance alternative forms of energy. The same scientific and technological developments were not, however, available to everyone. Yet international solidarity is a fundamental premise for full and balanced development.

Widespread opinion would see in population control a solution to the problem of the availability of resources. The Church is aware of the complexity of the reorganization of production and redistribution policies but account must be taken of widely differing regional situations. While some countries show a massive population increase, others have a dwindling, aging population. "Often it is precisely the latter countries, with their high level of consumption, which are most responsible for the pollution of the environment", precisely through their high level of consumption.[28] In the face of such a situation, to apply methods contrary to the true nature of the human person can end up causing tragic harm.

The Church therefore continues to uphold the principle of responsible parenthood, including the right and responsibility of the spouses to decide the size of their family and the spacing of births, without pressures from governments or organizations. However, the question of population growth must be faced not by responsible parenthood alone but also by the availability of social and economic means in developing countries, among which education, professional training, improving the condition of

---

[27] Address to the Study Group of the Pontifical Academy of Sciences, 22 November 1991, No. 2.
[28] *Ibid.* No. 4

women, lowering infant mortality, and the improvement of the quality of life. These measures would also have to be accompanied by a redistribution of economic resources.

Finally, population is only one component in and rarely the primary cause of environmental degradation. On the other hand, the populations of the North are directly or indirectly responsible for most environmental abuse. True solutions to such problems involve not only sound economic planning and transfer of technology but justice for all the peoples of the earth.[29]

Defense of the poor

The Social Teaching of the Church consistently gives preferential attention to the situation of the poor. This was evident in the contribution of the Holy See throughout the Rio Conference. The Holy See upheld the duty to respect not only the liberty and human dignity of all peoples but also their social, cultural and religious traditions.

Structural forms of poverty must continue to be addressed, including lack of employment, of educational opportunities, of adequate primary health care.[30] The poor must not be singled out for population control measures as if it were the poor who by their very existence and number were the cause, rather than the victims, of a lack of development or ecological degradation.[31]

The environmental impact of war

The question of the relationship between war and the environment was also raised during this period. In papal teaching, in the case of war, it is always the human tragedy that dominates. The loss of innocent lives is unacceptable. At the same time, the environmental damage caused by war cannot be overlooked. It has serious consequences for all.

In the early days of the Gulf crisis, Pope John Paul II had spoken out

[29] Pro-memoria, 25 May 1992, No. 9.

[30] Archbishop Martino, Address of 3 June 1992, No. III and Cardinal Sodano, Address of 13 June, No. 6.

[31] Declaration of the Director of the Press Office of the Holy See, No. 2. Cf. Archbishop Martino, Address of 4 June 1992, No. III and Cardinal Sodano, Address of 13 June, No. 6.

several times hoping that the outbreak of war could be avoided. He noted that, even in limited military operations, the cost in human life would be high " to say nothing of the ecological, political, economic and strategic consequences... ".[32] Moreover, while environmental damage disrupts society and the life of peoples. It also harms the earth itself, and many people depend on the well-being of the earth for their very life.

When speaking to a Study Group of the Pontifical Academy of Sciences on Population Problems, Pope John Paul II made explicit the link between the conservation of resources and peaceful coexistence. The conservation of resources presupposes peace, because wars are among the worst causes of environmental damage. In turn, living together in peace presupposes solidarity.[33] At the time of the preparations for the Conference, the Holy See referred back to the 1990 World Day of Peace Message which had spelled out the devastation of war on both the human and natural environment.[34] During the Conference itself, the Holy See Delegation spoke still more strongly stating that " the environment is devastated and development thwarted by the outbreak of wars, when internal conflicts destroy homes, fields and factories, when intolerable circumstances force millions of peoples desperately to seek refuge away from their lands... when the rights of the most vulnerable – women, children, the aged and the infirm – are neglected or abused ".[35] Peace is ultimately a question of the harmony of *all* of creation.

Part IV

Conclusion

Throughout this period, the thought of the Holy See had become increasingly integrated. The basic principles had by now been consistently set out and could be applied to a broad range of specific situations. It had

[32] Address to the Diplomatic Corps, 12 January 1991, No. 7. Cf. Angelus, 13 January 1991 which was a special appeal for peace in the Gulf, and Angelus, 27 January 1991.

[33] Address to the Study Group of the Pontifical Academy of Sciences, 22 November 1991, No. 7.

[34] Pro-memoria, No. 8 citing 1990 *WDP* No. 12.

[35] Archbishop Martino, Part III.

also become startlingly evident that the environmental question cut across almost all social questions. While care for all of God's creation is a moral imperative, the environmental issue is not an isolated issue. It is linked with or a component of almost every other social question. This is especially true of the right to development, which necessarily includes the right to a sound and healthy environment. Both share the aim of enhancing the quality of life.

The human person remains the central actor in the environmental question. This person both acts on and is acted upon by the environment but is alone responsible for the conscious care of a creation, the goods of which are for all. This universal destination of goods, of all goods, has now become a crucial social, political and economic issue.

At the end of the United Nations Conference on Environment and Development, Cardinal Sodano quoted John Paul II's Encyclical *Centesimus Annus*. It is an apt conclusion to this period:

> Not only has God given the earth to man, who must use it with respect for the original good purpose for which it was given to him, but man too is God's gift to man. He must therefore respect the natural and moral structure with which he has been endowed.[36]

Part V

Overview from 1990 through June 1992

1. *General Considerations*

- The human person is central to all considerations as regards both development and care for the environment.
- The present destruction of the environment is only one aspect of a profound moral crisis.
- The maintaining of a sound and healthy environment for all requires carefully coordinated solutions that are based on a morally coherent worldview.

[36] *CA* No. 38.

- A balance must be maintained between the demands of progress and the conservation of the natural patrimony.
- The richer countries must take a serious look at their lifestyle, which is consuming an inordinate share of the goods of the earth.
- In much of modern society, there is a type of social selfishness in which the needs of the other are ignored.

2. *The environmental question: its overall nature and components*

- The environmental question is transversal and relational and is a component in almost all social issues.
- It is relational, concerning:
  - relations with the Creator and a sensitivity to God's will for all of creation;
  - relations with others, that is the societal aspect of care for creation for the good of all;
  - relations with the natural world, a good in itself.
- Peace, the common good of life in society and among societies, is related to care for the environment. War threatens this care for the environment and also leads to a disruption in the balance of nature.
- As regards the protection of the environment, the complex and widely diverse question of population growth is one factor among several to be taken into consideration.
- In all considerations concerning environmental protection, particular attention must be paid to the needs of the poor and the promotion of their good.
- Structural forms of poverty must be addressed.

3. *Selected moral principles*

- The universal destination of created goods:
  - The goods of creation are for all, including future generations.
  - These goods include not only natural goods but also the fruit of human activity.

- The few cannot destroy the environment or exhaust its resources when they are for all.

- A new solidarity is now called for that takes into consideration not only the needs of all people but also the protection of the environment in view of the good of all.

- Great care must be taken in any form of genetic manipulation, which must be ruled by ethical norms.

Chapter Five

EXPANDING AND DEEPENING THE VISION

1992 through 1999

In the period following the Rio Conference, the moral obligation to care for the environment is increasingly presumed. Environmental degradation continues to be cited as one of the major problems facing the world today. This period is also one during which specific topics are increasingly addressed.

Part I examines a significant number of Encyclicals and Apostolic Exhortations, while Part II considers the centrality of the human person, a key question that had also been recognized by the Rio Conference. Part III takes up some specific questions of increasing urgency while Part IV looks at how the person relates to the natural world. Five years after the Rio Conference, there was a brief international review of the situation. This is dealt with in Part V, while Part VI concludes the chapter. Because they have already been so well established, no overview of the dominant principles of this period is given.

Part I

The Environment: An All-Embracing Concern

Encyclical Letters

In the years following the Rio Conference, major papal Encyclicals and Apostolic Exhortations continued to refer to the obligation to care for the environment.[1] Life in all its dimensions is the focus of the Encyclical *Evangelium Vitae*.[2] In Pope John Paul II's vision, this includes care for the environment. He therefore welcomed the growing attention being paid to

---

[1] The Apostolic Letter *Tertio Millennio Adveniente*, issued in November 1994, traced a program for the preparation for the Jubilee of the Year 2000. It will be dealt with in the next chapter, dedicated to this Jubilee and the succeeding years.

[2] Encyclical Letter *Evangelium Vitae*, 25 March 1995, Nos. 27, 35, 42. [Text Fifteen]

ecology, a question he declared closely related to life. This was especially true in the more developed societies where attention was now also increasingly turning to the quality of life.[3] As God's living images, the human community is, moreover, called to defend and promote life, to show reverence and love for it. This includes a specific responsibility for creation that ranges from the preservation of natural habitats of animals and other forms of life to what is called "human ecology". "When it comes to the natural world, we are subject not only to biological laws but also to moral ones, which cannot be violated with impunity".[4]

Environment also finds its place in the Encyclical *Fides et Ratio* concerning the complex relationship between faith and reason in modern times.[5] When faced with the many contemporary challenges in social, economic, political and scientific fields, the ethical conscience of people has often become disoriented. The role of truth is fundamental. Yet, there is at present a crisis of truth and consequently need for an ethics that looks to the truth of the good. This in turn calls for a moral theology that implies both a philosophical anthropology and a metaphysics of good. Such an organic vision would allow persons to tackle effectively the many problems related to peace, social justice, the family, the defense of life and the natural environment.[6] It would also provide a potent underpinning "for the true and planetary ethics which the world now needs".[7] This call for a global ethics is complementary to John Paul II's ongoing insistence on the need for a morally coherent world vision.[8]

Apostolic Exhortations

In the years between 1995 and 1999, Pope John Paul II issued three documents[9] that both followed up on and reflected the discussions of a

[3] *EV* No. 27.

[4] *EV* No. 47, referring to *SRS* No. 34.

[5] Encyclical Letter *Fides et Ratio*, 14 September 1998, Nos. 98, 104. [Text Sixteen]

[6] *FR* No. 92. This carefully reasoned question is only very briefly summarized here. It would be important to refer to the texts of both No. 92 and No. 104.

[7] *FR* No. 104.

[8] 1990 *WDP* No. 1. Cf. among others, Address to the Ambassador of New Zealand, 14 November 1992.

[9] The Post-Synodal Apostolic Exhortation *Vita Consecrata*, 25 March 1996, No. 90, developed the relationship between evangelical poverty, to which men and women religious

series of Synods of Bishops that considered the life of a universal Church within specific continental boundaries. Three of these Apostolic Exhortations dealt with the environmental questions affecting such vast and diverse regions as America,[10] Asia,[11] and Oceania.[12] It is interesting to note the diversity of approaches and specific problems addressed.

The Apostolic Exhortation *Ecclesia in America* raised the question of the effects of the globalization process which has significant repercussions in America. On the one hand, globalization brings with it greater efficiency and increased productivity. It also forges economic links among different countries. It therefore has the potential of leading to greater unity among peoples. On the other hand, if the process is ruled merely by the laws of the market applied to suit the powerful, the negative results can include, among other, the destruction of the environment and natural resources.[13]

In directly addressing questions of ecological concern, the focus of the text is clearly on responsibility and obligations, the fulfillment of which supposes an openness to a spiritual and ethical perspective "capable of overcoming selfish attitudes and ' lifestyles which lead to the depletion of natural resources ' ". [14] How much ecological abuse and destruction there is in many parts of America, for example emissions of harmful gases and the phenomenon of forest fires sometimes even set deliberately. Devasta-

---

are committed, and care for the environment through simplicity of life and a preferential love for the poor. Because it is addressed to such a specific group within the Catholic Church, it is not considered here. Since, however, it deals with the relationship of evangelical poverty, to which all are called, and the use of the earth's resources, the relevant passage is included among the accompanying texts. [Text Seventeen]

[10] This Synod linked North and South America, thus forming a unit of peoples of different cultures and languages, and historical, political and economic contexts facing interrelated problems. The Apostolic Exhortation *Ecclesia in America* was issued on 22 January 1999. Cf. Nos. 20, 25. [Text Eighteen]

[11] The Apostolic Exhortation *Ecclesia in Asia,* 6 November 1999, No. 41. [Text Nineteen]

[12] The Apostolic Exhortation *Ecclesia in Oceania,* 22 November 2001, Nos. 28, 31. While this Exhortation was published in 2001, the Synod itself took place in the period under consideration. It will therefore be considered together with the two other geographically based Synods mentioned. [Text Twenty]

[13] *EA* No. 20.

[14] *Ibid.* No. 25. The internal quotation reflects one of the Propositions adopted by the Synod.

tions such as these could lead to growing desertification with subsequent increased hunger and misery. The preservation of the vast Amazonian forest, which extends into several countries, is an urgent problem, because its biodiversity makes it vital for the environmental balance of the entire planet.[15]

Different environmental concerns face the Asian region where economic and technical progress has not been accompanied by concern for the balance of the ecosystem. This disrespect for the environment will continue as long as the earth and its potential are seen as objects of immediate use and consumption in an unbridled desire for profit. Christians, together with all, must restore a sense of reverence for the whole of God's creation. The Synod for Asia stressed the responsibility of the leaders of nations, legislators and business people in managing the earth's resources and the importance of education to stewardship, especially for the young, but also in view of future generations.[16]

The document issued after the Synod concerning the vast region of Oceania, *Ecclesia in Oceania,* spoke of its great natural beauty. The region still offers to indigenous peoples a place to live in harmony with nature and with one another. The Australian aborigines are, however, struggling to survive. After having sought for centuries to live in harmony with their often-harsh environment, they are now faced with the loss of their identity and culture despite significant measures taken. The Church will support the cause of all indigenous peoples who seek just and equitable recognition of their identity and their aspirations for a just solution to the question of the alienation of their lands.[17]

In Oceania, the concrete problems stemming from the harmful policies of some of the industrialized countries and transnationals include deforestation, pollution of rivers by mining, over-fishing and fouling of fishing grounds with industrial and nuclear waste. This latter is a danger to human health. At the same time, it must not be forgotten that industry can bring great benefits to the region if it respects the rights and cultures of the peoples and the integrity of the environment.

[15] *Ibid.*
[16] *Ecclesia in Asia* No. 41.
[17] *EO* Nos. 28, 31.

The vast panorama that these Synod documents traced brings out clearly the importance of the Social Teaching of the Church in the field of the environment. The key concepts remain the centrality of the human person and the universal destination of all created goods, including those due to human activity.[18]

Part II

The Post-Rio Period: the Centrality
of the Human Person in Creation

In the 1990 World Day of Peace Message *Peace with God, Peace with All of Creation,* Pope John Paul II had emphasized the need for carefully coordinated solutions, based on a morally coherent world vision, to the environmental crisis. In this context, the role of the human person in protecting and renewing the environment remains central. The Rio Declaration adopted by the United Nations Conference on the Environment and Development had moreover recognized this, stating that "Human beings are at the centre of concerns for sustainable development. They are entitled to a healthy and productive life in harmony with nature".[19]

While part of creation, human persons have a special place within the world.[20] Not only do they use its resources; God entrusted it to their care. They must always keep in mind that they are part of creation and never set out to destroy it.[21] Their special place within creation "lies in their being

---

[18] An Apostolic Letter *Orientale Lumen* was issued on 2 May 1995. Which recognizes the age-old contribution of the Oriental Churches to the one Church of Christ. It makes explicit the interesting relationship that exists between liturgical prayer and the cosmic reality, also called to give thanks, and respect for creation. Cf. No. 11.

[19] *Rio Declaration*, Principle 1.

[20] The centrality of the human person continued to dominate papal thought on the environment in the succeeding years. Its contours are so well established that only a brief mention will be made of it here to bring to completion current papal thought on this question.

[21] Address to the Bishops of North Western Germany, 14 December 1992, No. 13.

given *a share in God's own concern and providence for the whole of creation*".[22]

In considering the relationship of the human person to the preservation of the environment, three aspects of the nature of the human person must be taken into account. This person is an individual, a member of society, and a steward of creation.[23] These three coordinates situate the place of the human person within creation. It is a question of relationship, colored by responsibility, but also conditioned by limits. The most fundamental of these limits is a recognition of the radical otherness of God. If it is true that God is in the world and that he has a certain immanence, he is transcendent, "above the world", and cannot be identified with it.[24] The world is a gift of God the Creator, who is love, while the human person is a creature called to responsible stewardship.[25] There is, however, an immense dignity to this stewardship which means that the person actually collaborates with God through his or her work and intelligence.[26]

The second limit comes from God's having destined the goods of this earth for the good of all. Everyone without exception is invited to the table of creation, the goods of which either come directly from the hands of the Creator or are the result of human activity.[27] When they are not equitably shared, it is above all the poor who suffer.[28]

This universal destination of created goods obviously calls into question any development model that harms the environment or does not favor the integral development of the poorer sectors of society, and of the poorer countries within the world community.[29] It also requires taking very seriously the implications of the moral virtue of solidarity by

[22] Address on the World Day of Youth, 14 August 1993, Denver, Colorado, Part I, No. 2.

[23] Address to the Diplomatic Corps, 10 January 1998, No. 3.

[24] Homily at the closing Mass of the Synod of Asia, 14 May 1998.

[25] Address to the Rectors of Academic Institutions, Torn, Poland, 7 June 1999, No. 6.

[26] Lenten Message for 1992, dated 29 June 1991. Cf. among others, Address on the occasion of the St. Francis International Prize, 22 October 1992; Angelus, 24 March 1996.

[27] Lenten Message for 1992.

[28] Lenten Message for 1994, signed 3 September 1993, No. 5.

[29] Cf. among others, Address to the European Bureau for the Environment, 7 June 1996, No. 2 and Address to the Ambassador of Mauritius, 24 April 1997 which states that integral human development is essential to peace.

which all are really responsible for the good of all.[30] The richer nations are consuming an excessive amount of the goods of the earth. This calls not only for a profound change in their typical consumer lifestyle,[31] but also legal guarantees concerning the responsible management of the earth's resources.[32]

Part III
Specific Social Questions

The now well-established moral basis for the consideration of the environmental crisis led Pope John Paul II to turn increasingly to very specific questions. From among the many he addresses only those related to food production, water and chemical hazards are considered here. All condition the possibility of integral development as well as the promotion of a safe environment.

Food Production

This critical question is related to the rural development of an increasingly urbanized world. It affects all those who work the land or distribute its fruits. Despite a sufficient production capacity, people are dying from hunger across the world, at times because their peace and security are not guaranteed, at others because the goods of the earth are not shared in a rational way.[33] Sound food production requires, in the first place, access to land and the protection of the rights of the agricultural worker.

Food security has become a new concept in food production and distribution. It considers the availability of food not only in relation to the

---

[30] Cf. *SRS* No. 38.

[31] Cf. among others, 1999 World Day of Peace Message, No. 10.

[32] Address to the Ambassador of New Zealand, 14 November 1992. Cf. also, among others, 1999 *WDP* No. 10.

[33] Address to the XXVIII Session of the Conference of FAO, 23 November 1995, No 3.

needs of a given country but also in relation to the production capacity of neighboring areas, with a view to its rapid transfer or exchange in times of need.[34] This is a living example of solidarity in act.

Recent developments have also led to efforts to limit damage to the ecosystem and to safeguard food-producing regions from desertification and erosion. Attempts are also being made to facilitate the sharing of the goods of the earth. The Holy Father has recognized the role of the Food and Agriculture Organization in leading the way in this difficult field.[35]

Water

An adequate supply of fresh water across the world is now considered one of the major problems facing the future. Pope John Paul II had already addressed the question when he visited the Sahel. In his 1993 Lenten Message, he did not hesitate to develop the biblical aspect, citing the frequent references of Jesus to water and to thirst.[36]

Water is essential to life and countless men and women suffer from the tragic desertification of their lands due to its lack. At times, human activity is the cause of the barrenness of the land and the pollution of clean water. This must stop, because entire peoples have been reduced to destitution and disease because of the lack of clean drinking water. Rain patterns also seem to be changing because of uncontrolled industrial development. The solutions to such serious problems can only be found through cooperation and the generous support of those agencies that are helping people to fight this scourge.[37] The peoples of Oceania have a special responsibility to assume on behalf of humanity: stewardship of the Pacific Ocean that contains over half of the earth's total supply of water.[38] There is an obvious link between an adequate water supply and development.

---

[34] *Ibid.* No. 5.
[35] *Ibid. passim.*
[36] Cf. for example *Jn* 4: 7, *Mt* 10: 42, *Mt* 25: 34-35.
[37] Lenten Message for 1993 *passim.*
[38] *EO* No. 31.

Chemical Hazards

Who, the Holy Father asks, cannot but be deeply concerned by the prospect of the already existing and ever expanding danger of pollution from the production and use of chemicals?[39] This is a problem which especially strikes the developing countries that do not as yet have in place all the necessary regulations and infrastructures to assure safety in this field. "It is a serious abuse and an offense against human solidarity when industrial enterprises in the richer countries profit from the economic and legislative weaknesses of poorer countries to locate production plants or accumulate waste which will have a degrading effect on the environment and on people's health".[40]

The solution is not to deny developing countries the imports and technologies they need and which often have to do with food production. This question cannot, moreover, be divorced from the ethical and moral character of development.

Respect for the natural environment and the correct and moderated use of the resources of creation are part of each individual's moral obligations to others. "It would be difficult to overstate the weight of *the moral duty incumbent on developed countries to assist the developing countries in their efforts to solve their chemical pollution and health hazard problems.*[41] The right to a safe environment is also increasingly presented as a right to include in an updated Charter of Human Rights".[42]

The human family is at a crossroads in its relationship to the natural environment. Not only must there be increased efforts at solidarity, it is also necessary to insist on the interdependence of the various ecosystems and the importance of their balance for human survival.[43]

---

[39] Address to a Study Group of the Pontifical Academy of Sciences on Chemical Hazards in Developing Countries, 22 October 1993.

[40] *Ibid*. No. 2.

[41] *Ibid*. No. 3.

[42] *Ibid*. No. 4 quoting the 1990 World Day of Peace Message, No. 9.

[43] *Ibid*. No. 5.

Part IV

A Relationship with Nature

In this period of consolidation and deepening of the social thought of the Church as regards the environment, by far the richest contribution is the attention paid to our relationship with the natural world as a mirror of God.

Nature as revealing God

Anyone who wants to find self must learn to savor nature, the beauty of which is linked to the silence of contemplation. In fact, the rhythms of creation are so many paths of extraordinary beauty along which the believing heart can grasp the beauty of God the Creator.[44] If one is attentive to the attitude of Jesus, one can grasp his own contemplative attitude before the wonders of creation.[45]

People can learn to see the Creator by contemplating the beauty of his creatures; the human person can discover the Artist's hand in his wonderful works. Reason can also know God through the book of nature: a personal God who transcends the world but at the same time is present in the depths of his creatures. "If you look at the world with a pure heart, you too will see the face of God (cf. *Mt* 5: 8), because it reveals God's provident love".[46] We must not, however, confuse the Creator with creation.

The language of nature

Nature also has its own language that must be learned. It is only by withdrawing from the often frantic rhythm of the cities, that we can listen to that new language of nature that raises the human person to the heights

---

[44] Angelus at Santo Stefano di Cadore, Italy, 7 July 1993.

[45] Homily at Santo Stefano di Cadore, Italy, 11 July 1993. This homily develops the relationship of Jesus as Word to creation and the call of the human person as regards the salvation of creation.

[46] Address to Youth, World Day of Youth, 14 August 1993, Denver, Colorado, Part II, No. 5-6.

of mystery. To do so, we must create silence within and around ourselves in order to allow this language to speak to our hearts and learn to decipher this interior language of nature.[47]

Part V

The Activity of the Holy See – Rio + Five

During this period, the Holy See continued to follow a significant number of meetings that dealt with environmental questions. The most important of these, however, was its participation in Rio + Five, the 19th Special Session of the General Assembly of the United Nations, held in New York from 23 to 28 June 1997. The purpose of the Special Session was to assess progress in implementing *Agenda 21*, the final document of the 1992 Rio Conference. The very brevity of the meeting is indicative of the difficulties that States had met in implementing its various concrete measures.

The Statement of the Holy See briefly summarized its points of concern at that time,[48] and noted that the results obtained at Rio had made it a duty to protect nature in order to defend humanity. This had to be done in a spirit of solidarity, without underestimating the links between ecology, economics and equitable development. The problem of displaced persons, over fifty million at that time, who had left their homes and lands as a result of no assurance of human or economic security was also underscored. The needs of these people cannot be forgotten.

Another important question is that of education to respect for nature and a wise use of the earth's resources. Such an education would help young people to develop attitudes of acceptance, sharing and giving. Believers should also wish to help men and women to go beyond mere respect for nature and rediscover a sense of awe before the beauty of nature that raises us to the Creator. It suffices to think not only of the Can-

[47] Address to Italian ski instructors, 3 May 1993, No. 2.

[48] Archbishop Tauran, Secretary of the Second Section of the Secretariat of State, also pointed out those aspects of the proposed final documents of Rio + 5 that dealt with "reproductive health", "sexual health" and "family planning". These topics had once again been raised in a document dedicated to care for the environment.

ticle of the Sun of Francis of Assisi but also of the phrase of Teilhard de Chardin on the spiritual power of matter which Pope Paul VI had referred to as early as 1971.[49] Finally, the Holy See hoped that all would "follow the path of participation, discussion and perseverance".[50] The environmental crisis still remains, in fact, a problem that must be addressed by all.

Part VI

Conclusion

During this period of consolidation and development, the moral and theological concepts consistently referred to previously assumed less importance and were taken as a given. This span of years was, however, rich in thought and brought out the importance of the participation of all, even through small measures.

As in the past, Pope John Paul II makes explicit the relationship between faith, values, and behavior. An appreciation of the beauty of creation seems almost inevitably to open the mind to the original harmony that God still intends for what is actually, we now know, a small part of creation. It also leads to a greater sense of the need to care for creation in an active and responsible way. This holds for the individual but can also be true for society. An education to this aspect of the human relationship to creation is becoming more difficult in an increasingly urbanized world where the human person has little contact with nature.

The obligation to care for the environment has serious social consequences. Pope John Paul II, addressing the General Assembly of the Pontifical Council for Justice and Peace,[51] dedicated precisely to the question of the environment, did not hesitate to say:

[49] Address to the International Institute of Juridical Studies, 27 March 1971.

[50] Statement of the Holy See to the Rio + 5 Special Session of the General Assembly of the United Nations, 27 June 1997.

[51] 4 November 1999.

Reflecting on the environment in the light of Sacred Scripture and the Social Teaching of the Church, we cannot but raise the question of the very style of life promoted by modern society, and in particular the question of the uneven way in which the benefits of progress are distributed. The Pontifical Council will render a valuable service to the Church, and through the Church to all of humanity, in promoting a deeper understanding of the obligation to work for greater justice and equity in the way people are enabled to share in the resources of God's creation.

Chapter Six

A NEW MILLENNIUM: TOWARDS THE FUTURE

2000 leading into 2002

The concluding period of this historical overview is marked by two occurances: the beginning of a new millennium, opening up to a future of hope, but also the continuance of conflicts that are compounded by an increase in terrorism. While care for the environment was one of the basic themes of both the preparation for and celebration of the Jubilee Year in the Church, other concerns began to dominate. Yet, during the short post-Jubilee period, the well-established moral principles concerning care for the environment continue to be presented in fresh ways.

In this concluding chapter, Part I is limited to the Jubilee period while Part II presents the specific challenge of the agricultural world. Part III is dedicated to two singular documents. The first is the Holy See's contribution to the 2002 United Nations World Summit for Sustainable Development, thirty years after the Stockholm Conference. The second document marks a new phase in the development of an ethical code for the environment. In June 2002, His Holiness John Paul II joined His All Holiness Bartholomew I, the Ecumenical Patriarch of Constantinople, in signing a joint declaration on care for the environment. Two clear and strong voices in defense of the environment thus spoke as one.

Part I

The Celebration of the Jubilee of the Year 2000

The earth as gift of God to all

In the biblical tradition, the Jubilee Celebration was fundamentally oriented towards the re-establishment of right relationships, above all, those of a people with God. However, justice was also to be restored among people and to include such concrete measures as the freeing of slaves, the canceling of debts, the restoration of property. It also was a reminder that the earth was a gift to be cared for and developed by the human persons who were to act not as owners of the land but "as strangers and sojourners" (*Lev* 25: 23). The earth and its fruits had been given to all, not to the few; hence special attention was due to the poor. Across the centuries, this same Jubilee spirit was maintained ideally if not always in practice. It was to be prominent in the celebration of the Jubilee of the Year 2000.

Apostolic Letters and the Papal Bull

In 1994, Pope John Paul II had presented a carefully articulated three-year program of preparation leading up to the year 2000.[1] It was clear that the biblical relationship of Jubilee to social questions would be one of the basic elements of the preparation and subsequent celebration of the Jubilee. Pride of place would be given to the poor and the vulnerable in a celebration meant to restore equality among all.[2] If the precise prescriptions of the biblical Jubilee Year had historically remained largely ideals, they looked to the future, towards a time when social justice would actually be restored.[3]

In this eschatological perspective, the basic attitude was one of a hope that gives meaning and value to life. Among the signs of such hope in today's world – signs that at times remain hidden – are: the immense progress in scientific technological and medical fields at the service of human life, a greater awareness of our responsibility for the environment, and efforts to restore peace and justice wherever they are violated.[4] Care for the environment continues, therefore, to be seen as an essential element in the establishment of a justice and peace that are so needed in today's world.

Incarnationis Mysterium, the solemn announcement of the Jubilee Celebration of the Year 2000,[5] stated that to realize these eschatological hopes, all must accept responsibility for the development of an economic

---

[1] Apostolic Letter *Tertio Millennio Adveniente*, 10 November 1994, No. 13, 46. Cf. No. 6. [Text Twenty-One]

[2] *TMA* No. 13.

[3] *Ibid.*

[4] *Ibid.* No. 46.

[5] Bull of Indiction of the Great Jubilee of the Year 2000 *Incarnationis Mysterium*, No. 12. [Text Twenty-Two]

model that serves the good of all. It is clear that "extreme poverty is a source of violence, bitterness and scandal".[6] To make the necessary changes is clearly difficult, calling for the participation of all sectors of society. However, the Jubilee approaches the question from another perspective and calls for a conversion of heart through a change of life. The earth belongs to God and to him alone.[7]

At the end of the Jubilee Year, Pope John Paul II issued another Apostolic Letter *Novo Millennio Ineunte* in order to carry the spirit of the Jubilee into the new millennium. The Jubilee was not to be a passing celebration but must become an integral part of Christian life. In this light, "how can we remain indifferent to the prospect of an *ecological crisis* which is making vast areas of our planet uninhabitable and hostile to humanity? ... Countless are the emergencies to which every Christian heart must be sensitive".[8]

Part II

The Goods of Creation Are For All: A Challenge for the Agricultural World

In the recent social thought of the Church, at least from the time of Pope Pius XII, particular attention has been paid to the problems of the agricultural sector. Care for the land remains one of the more important elements in environmental considerations.[9] Those who work the land

---

[6] *Ibid.*

[7] *Ibid.*

[8] Apostolic Letter *Novo Millennio Ineunte*, No. 51. This call to care for the earth must be situated within John Paul II's request for a compassionate response to the contradictions of a world in which the few have immense possibilities while millions of others are in conditions far below the minimum demanded by human dignity. In every Christian community the poor must feel at home. Cf. *NMI* No. 50; 2001 *WDP* No. 17 and Address to the Diplomatic Corps, 13 January 2001, No. 13.

[9] Cf. among others, Pius XII, Address to the First International Catholic Congress on the Problems of Rural Life, 2 July 1951, *Discorsi*, Vol. XIII, p. 195; Address to the International Federation of Farmers, 10 June 1953, *Discorsi,* Vol. XV, p. 200; Address to the Italian National Federation of Farmers, 18 May 1955, *Discorsi*, Vol. XVII, p. 95.

have a particular relationship to the soil and natural elements that influences the entire food production process. They also often face immense challenges in the distribution of the fruits of their work. At the same time, rural peoples have, at times, either abused the land, or been victims of its abuse. In an increasingly urbanized world, the problems of the agricultural world can also be pushed to the margins. Yet this sector plays a crucial role in a balanced world environment and integral development. During the Jubilee Year, Pope John Paul II presented an ample teaching in this regard.

An overview of the problems that the agricultural world faces today is indicative of the degree to which social disorders have consequences in other areas. In the natural order, farmers are often faced with disasters or climatic problems that can put their entire harvest at risk or result in drought or flooding. Actually, the greatest risk to food production comes, however, from human activity and, at times, is not directly connected with the rural world. Rampant industrialization, with the resultant air and water pollution and production of toxic wastes, directly affects the quality of air and of water sources. Uncontrolled urbanization patterns also encroach upon fertile lands or forest lands. Other serious problems are the result of human interference in the ecological balance of a region.[10]

Pope John Paul II also returns to the ever-present problem of violence. The degree to which war and internal conflicts affect the environment and in particular their destructive impact on the land itself is often overlooked. Wars are a major cause of disruption of both food production and distribution. The result is the aggravation of already serious hunger and malnutrition problems.[11] Far too often internal conflicts are actually " wars of the poor "[12] that destroy the very basis of existence of those many peoples who depend on farming. It is not enough, however, to attempt to solve the problems of the rural world in isolation. Their solution also depends on economic and political decisions that are often taken far from the rural world.

[10] Homily, Jubilee Mass for the Agricultural World, 12 November 2000, *L'Osservatore Romano*, Eng. edition, N. 46, p. 1, No. 3.

[11] Message to Mr. Diouf, Director General of FAO on the occasion of the World Food Day, 4 October 2000.

[12] Address on the occasion of the Jubilee Celebration of the Agricultural World, 11 November 2000, No. 5.

In today's world, the agricultural sector faces a series of macro-problems that arise from a globalizing economy to which they often have insufficient access and from a consumer society that fosters a culture of waste which does not take into account the availability of resources and the poverty of so many of the world's people.[13] The unequal distribution of the produce of the earth is due not only to poor distribution chains or to lack of access to world markets. As with other social problems, the food needs of a society of waste tax available resources resulting in unjust distribution patterns. There is a clear need on the part of the more developed countries to commit themselves to "a reasonably austere lifestyle" in order to help those who lack food.[14]

A very specific problem of modern scientific progress is that of the application of biotechnology to food production. The introduction of such techniques cannot be based on immediate economic interests but must rather be submitted to careful scientific and ethical examination. Human health and the very future of the earth could depend on decisions made in this field.[15]

Another serious question is that of the possible dangers of nuclear energy. This was brought to worldwide public awareness at the time of the accident in Chernobyl, which had "tragic and pitiless consequences for the environment and the lives of so many human beings".[16] The pollution of the land was extensive. Chernobyl has now become the symbol of the risks connected with nuclear energy. Every kind of energy must be put at the service of peace, respecting the needs of the human person and also of nature. A future without the fear of threats such as those of Chernobyl depends on such a commitment.[17]

The role that science can play in care for the environment is not always obvious. This was the case of the Eighth Vatican Observatory School in Astrophysics dedicated to a study of the final state of stars as they exhaust their normal sources of energy. In his Message to the participants in this School,[18] Pope John Paul II pointed out that this stellar phenomenon had

[13] *Ibid.* No. 8.

[14] Message to Mr. Diouf. Cf. 2001 *WDP* No. 17 and Address to the Diplomatic Corps, 13 January 2001, No. 5.

[15] Address on the occasion of the Jubilee Celebration of the Agricultural World, No. 4.

[16] Address at the Airport on arrival at Kiyev, Ukraine, 23 June 2001, No. 6.

[17] Address to Children from Chernobyl and their Hosts, 26 April 2001. Nos. 2, 4.

[18] 2 July 2001.

led them to examine some of the most fundamental aspects of the universe. Such a scientific effort to understand creation and the place of the human person within it was, in fact, one of the noblest human aspirations. Exploring the mysteries of the universe could benefit a fast-changing and troubled world. Research in the field of astrophysics is not remote from the daily concerns of people or irrelevant to the building of a more humane world. An empirically grounded vision of reality " leads to an understanding of the human person as an integral element in a created world ".[19]

Part III

On the Eve of the Johannesburg Conference

The Holy See's Paper to the IV Preparatory Committee Meeting for the World Summit for Sustainable Development

During the long period stretching from time of the Stockholm Conference of 1972 to the eve of the 2002 United Nations World Summit for Sustainable Development,[20] an interesting evolution has taken place in the titles of the series of United Nations Conferences. The first international conference dedicated to the environment had been entitled the *UN Conference on the Human Environment*. While the emphasis was clearly on care for the environment, the relationship between a sound environment and development was, as it were, an underlying leitmotif. An understanding of the role of the human person was key.

The Rio Conference of 1992 made the link between the environment and development explicit by entitling the meeting the *UN Conference on Environment and Development*. The coming 2002 Conference, *World Summit for Sustainable Development,* does not include the word environment in its title. Why this apparent lessening of attention to the environment? It could be that the environmental question has now become an

[19] *Ibid.*

[20] The World Summit for Sustainable Development, Johannesburg, South Africa, 26 August-4 September 2002.

essential component in development policy and planning. The transversal nature of the environmental question is also clearly recognized. The danger of this is that since the environmental factor is so present, care for the environment, the responsibility of all, could become that of no one.

An integrated approach was adopted in a paper that the Holy See submitted to the IV Preparatory Committee Meeting for the World Summit for Sustainable Development.[21] It notes that the World Summit will address *the three pillars of sustainable development* – the economic, the social and the environmental. The Holy See recognizes in this a sign of human solidarity on behalf of the common good which obviously includes the preservation of the earth's resources.[22] Human persons are in fact responsible not only to each other but also for the environment.[23] While much of this submission of the Holy See focuses specifically on development questions, care for the environment is considered throughout a *sine qua non* for integral and sustainable development.

In this regard, the document states that the conservation and sustainable use of natural resources is linked with the question of the large number of peoples who live in rural areas and whose needs are often overlooked. Their basic human needs cannot, however, be met without taking into consideration the environmental sustainability of their particular milieu. There is also a broader environmental question affecting development in all parts of the world, that of assuring adequate clean water for the world's population.[24] An incremental development policy must also be put in place by which the developing countries would integrate into their development plans environmental regulations that are in line with their national circumstances and possibilities.

The Venice Declaration

From as early as 1992, the Ecumenical Patriarch of the Greek Orthodox Church, His All Holiness Bartholomew I, has organized a series of studies, seminars and symposia on the environmental question. Represen-

---

[21] Bali, Indonesia, 27 May-7 June 2002.
[22] Paper of the Holy See to the IV Preparatory Committee Meeting for the World Summit for Sustainable Development. [Appendix One]
[23] *Ibid*. No. 3.
[24] *Ibid*. No. 5e.

tatives of the Holy See have participated fully in these various initiatives and have welcomed the leadership role of His All Holiness in this important field of mutual concern. In the preparatory phase of the IV Symposium on Religion, Science and the Environment organized under his patronage,[25] the decision was taken to draw up a Common Declaration on the environment to be signed by both Pope John Paul II and His All Holiness Bartholomew I. This Declaration would then be offered for consideration to the participants in the Johannesburg Conference.

On 10 June 2002, in the Ducal Palace of Venice, Bartholomew I and John Paul II signed a document now called the *Venice Declaration*.[26] The introductory passages situate their mutual concern for the environment in relation to the role of human persons, with their inalienable human dignity, in cooperating with God " in realizing more and more fully the divine purpose for creation ". Despite the continuing betrayal of the call to be stewards in watching over creation in holiness and wisdom, there is an encouraging growth in *ecological awareness*. This is none other than the acknowledgement of responsibility towards self, towards others, towards creation.

A solution to the present environmental degradation can only be found if a radical change of heart leads to a change in lifestyle and of unsustainable patterns of consumption and production. The children of the world are entitled to " a world free from degradation, violence and bloodshed, a world of generosity and love ".[27] Remains the need for an ethical code that would promote a true culture of life.

The Declaration invites all men and women of good will to ponder the importance of the following ethical goals:

1. To think of the world's children when considering our options for action.

2. To be open to study the true values that sustain every human culture.

[25] The first three Symposia on Religion, Science and the Environment, sponsored by the Ecumenical Patriarch of Constantinople studied the situation of the Aegean Sea, the Black Sea, and the Danube River. This IV Symposium on the Adriatic Sea was entitled " A Sea at Risk, a Unity of Purpose ". It took place on 5-10 June 2002.

[26] Pope John Paul II was linked with Venice by satellite. This allowed the two signatories to communicate with one another and all present in Venice to witness the mutual signing. The event was also televised worldwide. [Appendix Two]

[27] *Ibid.*

3. To use science and technology constructively, evaluating it in the light of the centrality of the human person, the common good, and the inner purpose of creation.

4. To be humble regarding ownership and open to the demands of solidarity.

5. To acknowledge the diversity of situations and responsibilities in work for a better world environment. Not every person and institution can assume the same burden.

6. To promote a peaceful approach to disagreement about how to live on this earth and about how to share and use it.[28]

The Declaration, which closes on a note of hope, is clear in its intent and in its realism. If taken seriously by the faithful of both Churches and by other men and women of good will, it could represent a solid basis for an environmental ethical code acceptable to a broad range of people.

Part IV

In Guise of Conclusion

Pope John Paul II had never hesitated to make explicit the relationship between a creation-based spirituality and care for the environment, that is for all of God's creation. He recently expressed what could be considered its quintessence in a series of reflections on the Psalms and other relevant biblical texts in which humanity is called to praise the Creator who reveals himself through the splendor and immensity of his works: "The heavens declare the glory of God. Day pours out the word to day and night to night imparts knowledge" (*Ps* 19: 2).

Nature speaks to us of God.[29] "The ear of the heart must be free of noise in order to hear this divine voice echoing in the universe... Nature

---

[28] *Ibid.* These goals are only briefly summarized. The text itself must be consulted.

[29] General Audience 26 January 2000, No. 5. Cf. *Wis* 13: 5, *Rm* 1: 20.

too, in a certain sense, is 'the book of God'".[30] One cannot but see the order that governs the cosmos and the dynamism that marks relations between the macrocosm and the microcosm.[31] This visionary and contemplative approach must however lead us to rediscover our kinship with the earth. "If nature is not violated and degraded, it once again becomes [our] sister".[32]

There can be no break between a deep and full appreciation of the wonder of God's creative act and the obligation to care for it in all its splendor and beauty, remembering that it was created for all, not for the few. John Paul II, therefore, does not hesitate to state that he must both support and encourage an "ecological conversion". People are actually becoming increasingly sensitive to the catastrophe to which humanity is heading. With this conversion, the original harmony would be rediscovered: the goods of the earth would be available to all, not just to the privileged few.[33]

The long period of development of papal teaching on the environment has reached its culmination. The contemplation of the wonders of nature has led Pope John Paul II to address an evermore urgent appeal to all to turn toward creation, to see in it the reflection of the Creator, and to assure that its fruits are for all. He does so in order that all may live in dignity and in beauty: the beauty of the harmony of a creation that is finally at peace.

---

[30] General Audience 2 August 2000, No. 3.
[31] *Ibid.* No. 3, No. 5.
[32] General Audience, 26 January 2000, No. 5.
[33] *Ibid.* No. 3-5 *passim.*

ANNEXES

Text One

Dogmatic Constitution on the Church
21 November 1964
Nos. 36, 41, 48

36. [extract] Christ, becoming obedient even unto death and because of this exalted by the Father,[1] entered into the glory of His kingdom. To Him all things are made subject until He subjects Himself and all created things to the Father that God may be all in all.[2] Now Christ has communicated this royal power to His disciples that they might be constituted in royal freedom and that by true penance and a holy life they might conquer the reign of sin in themselves.[3] Further, He has shared this power so that serving Christ in their fellow men they might by humility and patience lead their brethren to that King for whom to serve is to reign. But the Lord wishes to spread His kingdom also by means of the laity, namely, a kingdom of truth and life, a kingdom of holiness and grace, a kingdom of justice, love and peace.[4] In this kingdom creation itself will be delivered from its slavery to corruption into the freedom of the glory of the sons of God.[5] Clearly then a great promise and a great trust is committed to the disciples: " All things are yours, and you are Christ's, and Christ is God's ".[6]

The faithful, therefore, must learn the deepest meaning and the value of all creation, as well as its role in the harmonious praise of God. They must assist each other to live holier lives even in their daily occupations. In this way the world may be permeated by the spirit of Christ and it may more effectively fulfill its purpose in justice, charity and peace. The laity have the principal role in the overall fulfillment of this duty. Therefore, by their competence in secular training and by their activity, elevated from

---

[1] Cf. *Phil* 2: 8-9.
[2] Cf. *1 Cor* 15: 27-28.
[3] Cf. *Rm* 6: 12.
[4] From the *Preface* of the Feast of Christ the King.
[5] Cf. *Rm* 8: 21.
[6] Cf. *1 Cor* 3: 23.

within by the grace of Christ, let them vigorously contribute their effort, so that created goods may be perfected by human labor, technical skill and civic culture for the benefit of all men according to the design of the Creator and the light of His Word. May the goods of this world be more equitably distributed among all men, and may they in their own way be conducive to universal progress in human and Christian freedom. In this manner, through the members of the Church, will Christ progressively illumine the whole of human society with His saving light.

41. [extract] ... Finally, those who engage in labor-and frequently it is of a heavy nature- should better themselves by their human labors. They should be of aid to their fellow citizens. They should raise all of society, and even creation itself, to a better mode of existence. ...

48. [extract] ... The Church, to which we are all called in Christ Jesus, and in which we acquire sanctity through the grace of God, will attain its full perfection only in the glory of heaven, when there will come the time of the restoration of all things.[7] At that time the human race as well as the entire world, which is intimately related to man and attains to its end through him, will be perfectly reestablished in Christ.[8] ...

Text Two

GAUDIUM ET SPES

Pastoral Constitution on the Church in the Modern World
7 December 1965
Nos. 34, 36, 37, 57, 69

34. [extract] ... Throughout the course of the centuries, men have labored to better the circumstances of their lives through a monumental amount of individual and collective effort. To believers, this point is set-

[7] *Acts* 3: 21.
[8] Cf. *Eph* 1: 10; *Col* 1: 20; *Pet* 3: 10-13.

tled: considered in itself, this human activity accords with God's will. For man, created to God's image, received a mandate to subject to himself the earth and all it contains, and to govern the world with justice and holiness;[1] a mandate to relate himself and the totality of things to Him Who was to be acknowledged as the Lord and Creator of all. Thus, by the subjection of all things to man, the name of God would be wonderful in all the earth.[2]

This mandate concerns the whole of everyday activity as well. For while providing the substance of life for themselves and their families, men and women are performing their activities in a way which appropriately benefits society. They can justly consider that by their labor they are unfolding the Creator's work, consulting the advantages of their brother men, and are contributing by their personal industry to the realization history of the divine plan.[3]

36. Now many of our contemporaries seem to fear that a closer bond between human activity and religion will work against the independence of men, of societies, or of the sciences.

If by the autonomy of earthly affairs we mean that created things and societies themselves enjoy their own laws and values which must be gradually deciphered, put to use, and regulated by men, then it is entirely right to demand that autonomy. Such is not merely required by modern man, but harmonizes also with the will of the Creator. For by the very circumstance of their having been created, all things are endowed with their own stability, truth, goodness, proper laws and order. Man must respect these as he isolates them by the appropriate methods of the individual sciences or arts. Therefore if methodical investigation within every branch of learning is carried out in a genuinely scientific manner and in accord with moral norms, it never truly conflicts with faith, for earthly matters and the concerns of faith derive from the same God.[4] Indeed whoever labors to penetrate the secrets of

---

[1] Cf. *Gn* 1: 26-27; 9: 3; *Wis* 9: 3.
[2] Cf. *Ps* 8: 7 and 10.
[3] Cf. John XXIII, Encyclical Letter *Pacem in Terris*: AAS 55 (1963), p. 297.
[4] Cf. First Vatican Council, Dogmatic Constitution on the Catholic Faith, Ch. III: Denzinger 1785-1186 (3004-3005).

reality with a humble and steady mind, even though he is unaware of the fact, is nevertheless being led by the hand of God, who holds all things in existence, and gives them their identity. Consequently, we cannot but deplore certain habits of mind, which are sometimes found too among Christians, which do not sufficiently attend to the rightful independence of science and which, from the arguments and controversies they spark, lead many minds to conclude that faith and science are mutually opposed.[5]

But if the expression, the independence of temporal affairs, is taken to mean that created things do not depend on God, and that man can use them without any reference to their Creator, anyone who acknowledges God will see how false such a meaning is. For without the Creator the creature would disappear. For their part, however, all believers of whatever religion always hear His revealing voice in the discourse of creatures. When God is forgotten, however, the creature itself grows unintelligible.

37. [extract] ... Hence if anyone wants to know how this unhappy situation can be overcome, Christians will tell him that all human activity, constantly imperiled by man's pride and deranged self-love, must be purified and perfected by the power of Christ's cross and resurrection. For redeemed by Christ and made a new creature in the Holy Spirit, man is able to love the things themselves created by God, and ought to do so. He can receive them from God and respect and reverence them as flowing constantly from the hand of God. Grateful to his Benefactor for these creatures, using and enjoying them in detachment and liberty of spirit, man is led forward into a true possession of them, as having nothing, yet possessing all things.[6] "All are yours, and you are Christ's, and Christ is God's" (*1 Cor* 3: 22-23).

57. [extract] Christians, on pilgrimage toward the heavenly city, should seek and think of these things which are above.[7] This duty in no way

---

[5] Cf. Msgr. Pio Paschini, *Vita e opere di Galileo Galilei*, 2 volumes, Vatican Press (1964).

[6] Cf. *2 Cor* 6: 10.

[7] Cf. *Col* 3: 1-2.

decreases, rather it increases, the importance of their obligation to work with all men in the building of a more human world. Indeed, the mystery of the Christian faith furnishes them with an excellent stimulant and aid to fulfill this duty more courageously and especially to uncover the full meaning of this activity, one which gives to human culture its eminent place in the integral vocation of man.

When man develops the earth by the work of his hands or with the aid of technology, in order that it might bear fruit and become a dwelling worthy of the whole human family and when he consciously takes part in the life of social groups, he carries out the design of God manifested at the beginning of time, that he should subdue the earth, perfect creation and develop himself. At the same time he obeys the commandment of Christ that he place himself at the service of his brethren. ...

69. [extract] God intended the earth with everything contained in it for the use of all human beings and peoples. Thus, under the leadership of justice and in the company of charity, created goods should be in abundance for all in like manner.[8] Whatever the forms of property may be, as adapted to the legitimate institutions of peoples, according to diverse and changeable circumstances, attention must always be paid to this universal destination of earthly goods. In using them, therefore, man should regard the external things that he legitimately possesses not only as his own but also as common in the sense that they should be able to benefit not only him but also others.[9] On the other hand, the right of having a share of earthly goods sufficient for oneself and one's family belongs to everyone. The Fathers and Doctors of the Church held this opinion, teaching that men are obliged to come to the relief of the poor

---

[8] Cf. Pius XII, Encyclical *Sertum Laetitiae*: AAS 31 (1939), p. 642; John XXIII, Consistorial Allocution: AAS 52 (1960), pp. 5-11; John XXIII, Encyclical Letter *Mater et Magistra*: AAS 53 (1961), p. 411; First Vatican Council, Constitution on the Catholic Faith: Denzinger 1795, 1799 (3015, 3019). Cf. Pius XI, Encyclical Letter *Quadragesimo Anno*: AAS 23 (1931), p. 190.

[9] Cf. St. Thomas, *Summa Theologica*: II-II, q. 32, a. 5 ad 2; Ibid. q. 66, a. 2: cf. explanation in Leo XIII, Encyclical Letter *Rerum Novarum*: AAS 23 (1890-91) p. 651; cf. also Pius XII, Allocution of June 1, 1941: AAS 33 (1941), p. 199; Pius XII, Birthday Radio Address 1954: AAS 47 (1955), p. 27.

and to do so not merely out of their superfluous goods.[10] If one is in extreme necessity, he has the right to procure for himself what he needs out of the riches of others.[11] ...

Text Three

JUSTICE IN THE WORLD

Second Synod of Bishops
30 November 1971
Extracts

Chapter I, Para 2   Moreover, men are beginning to grasp a new and more radical dimension of unity; they perceive that their resources, as well as the precious treasures of air and water – without which there cannot be life – and the small delicate biosphere of the whole complex of all life on earth, are not infinite, but on the contrary must be saved and preserved as a unique patrimony belonging to all mankind.

Chapter I, Para. 4   Furthermore, such is the demand for resources and energy by the richer nations, whether capitalist or socialist, and such are the effects of dumping by them in the atmosphere and sea that irreparable

---

[10] Cf. St. Basil, Hom. in illud Lucae "Destruam horrea mea", n. 2 (PG 31, 263); Lactantius, Divinarum institutionum, lib. V. on justice (PL 6, 565 B); St. Augustine, In Ioann. Ev. tr. 50, n. 6 (PL 35, 1760); St. Augustine, Enarratio in Ps. CXLVII, 12 (PL 37, 192); St. Gregory the Great, Homiliae in Ev., hom. 20 (PL 76, 1165); St. Gregory the Great, Regulae Pastoralis liber, pars III c. 21 (PL 77 87); St. Bonaventure, In III Sent. d. 33, dub. 1 (ed Quaracchi, III, 728); St. Bonaventure, In IV Sent. d. 15, p. II, a. a q. 1 (ed. cit. IV, 371 b); q. de superfluo (ms. Assisi Bibl. Comun. 186, ff. 112a-113a); St. Albert the Great, In III Sent., d. 33, a.3, sol. 1 (ed. Borgnet XXVIII, 611); Id. In IV Sent. d. 15, a. 1 (ed. cit. XXIX, 494-497). As for the determination of what is superfluous in our day and age, cf. John XXIII, Radio-Television Message of Sept. 11, 1962: AAS 54 (1962) p. 682: "The obligation of every man, the urgent obligation of the Christian man, is to reckon what is superfluous by the measure of the needs of others, and to see to it that the administration and the distribution of created goods serve the common good".

[11] In that case, the old principle holds true: "In extreme necessity all goods are common, that is, all goods are to be shared". On the other hand, for the order, extension, and manner by which the principle is appplied in the proposed text, besides the modern authors: cf. St. Thomas, *Summa Theologica* II-II, q. 66, a. 7. Obviously, for the correct application of the principle, all the conditions that are morally required must be met.

damage would be done to the essential elements of life on earth, such as air and water, if their high rates of consumption and pollution, which are constantly on the increase, were extended to the whole of mankind.

Chapter I, Para. 5   The strong drive towards global unity, the unequal distribution which places decisions concerning three quarters of income, investment and trade in the hands of one third of the human race, namely the more highly developed part, the insufficiency of a merely economic progress and the new recognition of the material limits of the biosphere – all this makes us aware of the fact that in today's world new modes of understanding human dignity are arising.

Chapter III, Para. 25   We consider that we must also stress the new world-wide preoccupation which will be dealt with for the first time in the conference on human environment to be held in Stockholm in June 1972. It is impossible to see what right the richer nations have to keep up their claim to increase their own material demands, if the consequence is either that others remain in misery or that the danger of destroying the very physical foundations of life on earth is precipitated. Those who are already rich are bound to accept a less material way of life, with less waste, in order to avoid the destruction of the heritage which they are obliged by absolute justice to share with all other members of the human race.

Text Four

POPULORUM PROGRESSIO

Encyclical Letter of Pope Paul VI
26 March 1967
Nos. 22, 25, 27, 28

22. In the very first pages of Scripture we read these words: "Fill the earth and subdue it ".[1] This teaches us that the whole of creation is for man, that he has been charged to give it meaning by his intelligent activity, to complete and perfect it by his own efforts and to his own advantage.

---

[1] *Gn* 1: 28.

Now if the earth truly was created to provide man with the necessities of life and the tools for his own progress, it follows that every man has the right to glean what he needs from the earth. The recent Council reiterated this truth: "God intended the earth and everything in it for the use of all human beings and peoples. Thus, under the leadership of justice and in the company of charity, created goods should flow fairly to all".[2]

All other rights, whatever they may be, including the rights of property and free trade, are to be subordinated to this principle. They should in no way hinder it; in fact, they should actively facilitate its implementation. Redirecting these rights back to their original purpose must be regarded as an important and urgent social duty.

25. The introduction of industrialization, which is necessary for economic growth and human progress, is both a sign of development and a spur to it. By dint of intelligent thought and hard work, man gradually uncovers the hidden laws of nature and learns to make better use of natural resources. As he takes control over his way of life, he is stimulated to undertake new investigations and fresh discoveries, to take prudent risks and launch new ventures, to act responsibly and give of himself unselfishly.

27. The concept of work can turn into an exaggerated mystique. Yet, for all that, it is something willed and approved by God. Fashioned in the image of his Creator, "man must cooperate with Him in completing the work of creation and engraving on the earth the spiritual imprint which he himself has received".[3] God gave man intelligence, sensitivity and the power of thought – tools with which to finish and perfect the work He began. Every worker is, to some extent, a creator – be he artist, craftsman, executive, laborer or farmer.

Bent over a material that resists his efforts, the worker leaves his imprint on it, at the same time developing his own powers of persistence, inventiveness and concentration. Further, when work is done in common – when hope, hardship, ambition and joy are shared – it brings together and firmly unites the wills, minds and hearts of men. In its accomplishment, men find themselves to be brothers.[4]

---

[2] *Church in the World of Today*, No. 69: AAS 58 (1966) [cf. TPS *XI*, 306].

[3] Letter to the 51st Social Week at Lyon, in *Le travail et les travailleurs dans la société contemporaine*, Lyon: Chronique sociale (1965), 6.

[4] Cf., for example, M. D. Chenu, O.P., *Pour une théologie du travail*, Paris: Editions du Seuil (1955) [Eng. tr. *The Theology of Work*, Dublin: Gill, 1963].

28. Work, too, has a double edge. Since it promises money, pleasure and power, it stirs up selfishness in some and incites other to revolt. On the other hand, it also fosters a professional outlook, a sense of duty, and love of neighbor. Even though it is now being organized more scientifically and efficiently, it still can threaten man's dignity and enslave him; for work is human only if it results from man's use of intellect and free will.

Our predecessor John XXIII stressed the urgent need of restoring dignity to the worker and making him a real partner in the common task: "Every effort must be made to ensure that the enterprise is indeed a true human community, concerned about the needs, the activities and the standing of each of its members".[5]

Considered from a Christian point of view, work has an even loftier connotation. It is directed to the establishment of a supernatural order here on earth,[6] a task that will not be completed until we all unite to form that perfect manhood of which St. Paul speaks, "the mature measure of the fullness of Christ".[7]

Text Five

OCTOGESIMA ADVENIENS
Apostolic Letter of Pope Paul VI
14 May 1971
Nos. 9, 21

9. The inordinate growth of these centers accompanies industrial expansion, without being identified with it. Based on technological research and the transformation of nature, industrialization constantly goes forward, giving proof of incessant creativity. While certain

---

[5] Encyc. Letter *Mater et Magistra*: AAS 53 (1961), 423 [cf. TPS VII, 312].

[6] Cf., for example, O. von Nell-Breuning, S.J., *Wirtschaft und Gesellschaft*, vol. 1: Grundfragen, Freiburg: Herder (1956), 183-184.

[7] *Eph* 4: 13.

enterprises develop and are concentrated, others die or change their location. Thus new social problems are created: professional or regional unemployment, redeployment and mobility of persons, permanent adaptation of workers and disparity of conditions in the different branches of industry. Unlimited competition utilizing the modern means of publicity incessantly launches new products and tries to attract the consumer, while earlier industrial installations which are still capable of functioning become useless. While very large areas of the population are unable to satisfy their primary needs, superfluous needs are ingeniously created. It can thus rightly be asked if, in spite of all his conquests, man is not turning back against himself the results of his activity. Having rationally endeavored to control nature,[1] is he not now becoming the slave of the objects which he makes?

The environment

21. While the horizon of man is thus being modified according to the images that are chosen for him, another transformation is making itself felt, one which is the dramatic and unexpected consequence of human activity. Man is suddenly becoming aware that by an ill-considered exploitation of nature he risks destroying it and becoming in his turn the victim of this degradation. Not only is the material environment becoming a permanent menace – pollution and refuse, new illness and absolute destructive capacity – but the human framework is no longer under man's control, thus creating an environment for tomorrow which may well be intolerable. This is a wide-ranging social problem which concerns the entire human family.

The Christian must turn to these new perceptions in order to take on responsibility, together with the rest of men, for a destiny which from now on is shared by all.

---

[1] Encyclical Letter *Populorum Progressio*, 25: AAS 59 (1967), pp. 269-270.

MESSAGE OF POPE PAUL VI
TO THE STOCKHOLM CONFERENCE

Addressed to Mr. Maurice Strong, Secretary General

1 June 1972

A Hospitable Earth for Future Generations

On the occasion of the opening of the United Nations Conference on Environment, which you have prepared zealously and competently, we would like to tell you and all the participants of the interest with which we follow this great enterprise. The care of preserving and improving the natural environment, like the noble ambition of stimulating a first gesture of world co-operation in favour of this good necessary for everyone, meets needs that are deeply felt among the men of our times.

Today, indeed, there is a growing awareness that man and his environment are more inseparable than ever. The environment essentially conditions man's life and development, while man, in his turn, perfects and ennobles his environment through his presence, work and contemplation. But human creativeness will yield true and lasting fruit only to the extent to which man respects the laws that govern the vital impulse and nature's capacity for regeneration. Both are united, therefore, and share a common temporal future. So man is warned of the necessity of replacing the advance, often blind and turbulent, of material progress left to its dynamism alone, with respect for the biosphere in an overall vision of his domain, which has become " one Earth ", to quote the fine motto of the Conference.

The cancellation of distance by the progress of communication; the establishment of closer and closer bonds between the peoples through economic development; the growing subservience of the forces of nature to science and technology; the multiplication of human relations beyond the barriers of nationalities and races are so many factors of interdependence for better or for worse, for the hope of safety or the risk of disaster. An abuse, a deterioration in one part of the world has repercussions in other places and can spoil the quality of other people's lives, often unbeknown to themselves and through no fault of their own. Man now knows with absolute certainty that scientific and technical progress, despite its promising aspects for the advancement of all peoples, bears within it, like every human work, a heavy charge of ambivalence, for good and for evil.

In the first place intelligence can apply its discoveries as means of destruction, as in the case of atomic, chemical and bacteriological arms and so many other instruments of war, great and small, for which moral conscience can feel only horror. But how can we ignore the imbalances caused in the biosphere by the disorderly exploitation of the physical reserves of the planet, even for the purpose of producing something useful, such as the wasting of natural resources that cannot be renewed; pollution of the earth, water, the air and space, with the resulting attacks on vegetable and animal life? All that contributes to the impoverishment and deterioration of man's environment to the extent, it is said, of threatening his own survival. Finally, our generation must energetically accept the challenge of going beyond partial and immediate aims to prepare a hospitable earth for future generations.

Interdependency must now be met by joint responsibility; common destiny by solidarity. This will not be done by resorting to facile solutions. Just as the demographic problem is not solved by unduly limiting access to life, so the problem of the environment cannot be tackled with technical measures alone. The latter are indispensable, it is true, and your Assembly will have to study them and propose means to put the situation right. It is only too clear, for example, that industry being one of the main causes of pollution, it is absolutely necessary for those in charge of it to perfect their methods and find the means, as far as possible without harming production, to reduce, if not eliminate completely the causes of pollution. In this task of purification it is clear, too, that chemical research workers will play an important role, and that great hope is placed in their professional capacities.

But all technical measures would remain ineffectual if they were not accompanied by awareness of the necessity of a radical change of mentality. All are called to clear-sightedness and courage. Will our civilisation, tempted to increase its marvellous achievements by despotic domination of the human environment, discover in time the way to control its material growth, to use the earth's food with wise moderation, and to cultivate real poverty of spirit in order to carry out urgent and indispensable reconversions? We would like to think so, for the very excesses of progress lead

90

men, and, significantly, the young particularly, to recognise that their power over nature must be exercised in accordance with ethical demands. The saturation caused in some people by a life that is too easy and the growing awareness in a large number of the solidarity that links mankind, thus contribute to restoring the respectful attitude on which man's relationship with his environment is essentially based. How can we fail to recall here the imperishable example of St. Francis of Assisi and to mention the great Christian contemplative Orders, which offer the testimony of an inner harmony achieved in the framework of trusting communion with the rhythms and laws of nature?

"Everything created by God is good", the Apostle St. Paul writes (*1 Tim* 4: 4), echoing the text of Genesis that relates God's satisfaction with each of his works. To rule creation means for the human race not to destroy it but to perfect it; to transform the world not into a chaos no longer fit for habitation, but into a beautiful abode where everything is respected. So no one can take possession in an absolute and selfish way of the environment, which is not a "res nullius" – something not belonging to anyone – but the "res omnium" – the patrimony of mankind, so that those in possession of it – men in private or public life – must use it in a way that redounds to the real advantage of everyone. Man is certainly the first and truest treasure of the earth.

For this reason the care of offering everyone the possibility of access to a fair share in the resources, existing or potential, of our planet must weigh particularly on the conscience of men of goodwill. Development, that is, the complete growth of man, presents itself as *the* subject, the keystone of your deliberations, in which you will pursue not only ecological equilibrium but also a just equilibrium of prosperity between the centres of the industrialized world and their immense periphery. Want, it has rightly been said, is the worst of pollutions. Is it utopian to hope that the young nations, who are constructing, at the cost of great efforts, a better future for their peoples, seeking to assimilate the positive acquisitions of technical civilization, but rejecting its excesses and deviations, should become the pioneers in the building of a new world, for which the Stockholm Conference is called to give the starting signal? It would be all the more unfair to refuse them the means to do so, in that they have often had to pay a heavy, undeserved contribution to the degradation and impoverishment of the common biological patrimony. Thus, instead of seeing in the struggle for a better environment the reaction of fear of the rich, they would see in it, to the benefit of everyone, an dffirmation of faith and hope in the destiny of the human family gathered round a common project.

It is with these sentiments that we pray to the Almighty to grant to all the participants, together with the abundance of his Blessings, the light of Wisdom and the spirit of brotherly Love for the complete success of their work.

Text Seven

REDEMPTOR HOMINIS
Encyclical Letter of Pope John Paul II
4 March 1979
Nos. 8, 15, 16

8. [extract] *Redemption as a new creation* The Redeemer of the world! In him has been revealed in a new and more wonderful way the fundamental truth concerning creation to which the Book of Genesis gives witness when it repeats several times: "God saw that it was good".[1] The good has its source in Wisdom and Love. In Jesus Christ the visible world which God created for man[2] – the world that, when sin entered, "was subjected to futility"[3] – recovers again its original link with the divine source of Wisdom and Love. Indeed, "God so loved the world that he gave his only Son".[4] As this link was broken in the man Adam, so in the Man Christ it was reforged.[5] Are we of the twentieth century not convinced of the overpoweringly eloquent words of the Apostle of the Gentiles concerning the

[1] Cf. *Gn* 1 *passim.*
[2] Cf. *Gn* 1: 26-30.
[3] *Rm* 8: 20; cf. 8: 19-22; Vatican Council II, Pastoral Constitution on the Church in the Modern World *Gaudium et Spes*, 2, 13: *AAS* 58 (1966) 1026, 1034-1035.
[4] *Jn* 3: 16.
[5] Cf. *Rm* 5: 12-21.

"creation (that) has been groaning in travail together until now"[6] and "waits with eager longing for the revelation of the sons of God",[7] the creation that "was subjected to futility"? Does not the previously unknown immense progress – which has taken place especially in the course of this century – in the field of man's dominion over the world itself reveal – to a previously unknown degree – that manifold subjection "to futility"? It is enough to recall certain phenomena, such as the threat of pollution of the natural environment in areas of rapid industrialization, or the armed conflicts continually breaking out over and over again, or the prospectives of self-destruction through the use of atomic, hydrogen, neutron and similar weapons, or the lack of respect for the life of the unborn. The world of the new age, the world of space flights, the world of the previously unattained conquests of science and technology – is it not also the world "groaning in travail"[8] that "waits with eager longing for the revealing of the sons of God"?[9] ...

15. [extract] *What modern man is afraid of* Accordingly, while keeping alive in our memory the picture that was so perspicaciously and authoritatively traced by the Second Vatican Council, we shall try once more to adapt it to the "signs of the times" and to the demands of the situation, which is continually changing and evolving in certain directions.

The man of today seems ever to be under threat from what he produces, that is to say from the result of the work of his hands and, even more so, of the work of his intellect and the tendencies of his will. All too soon, and often in an unforeseeable way, what this manifold activity of man yields is not only subjected to "alienation", in the sense that it is simply taken away from the person who produces it, but rather it turns against man himself, at least in part, through the indirect consequences of its effects returning on himself. It is or can be directed against him. This seems to make up the main chapter of the drama of present-day human existence in its broadest and universal dimension. Man therefore lives increasingly in fear. He is afraid that what he produces – not all of it, of

---

[6] *Rm* 8: 22.
[7] *Rm* 8: 19.
[8] *Rm* 8: 22.
[9] *Rm* 8: 19.

course, or even most of it, but part of it and precisely that part that contains a special share of his genius and initiative – can radically turn against himself; he is afraid that it can become the means and instrument for an unimaginable self – destruction, compared with which all the cataclysms and catastrophes of history known to us seem to fade away. This gives rise to a question: Why is it that the power given to man from the beginning by which he was to subdue the earth[10] turns against himself, producing an understandable state of disquiet, of conscious or unconscious fear and of menace, which in various ways is being communicated to the whole of the present-day human family and is manifesting itself under various aspects?

This state of menace for man from what he produces shows itself in various directions and various degrees of intensity. We seem to be increasingly aware of the fact that the exploitation of the earth, the planet on which we are living, demands rational and honest planning. At the same time, exploitation of the earth not only for industrial but also for military purposes and the uncontrolled development of technology outside the framework of a long-range authentically humanistic plan often bring with them a threat to man's natural environment, alienate him in his relations with nature and remove him from nature. Man often seems to see no other meaning in his natural environment than what serves for immediate use and consumption. Yet it was the Creator's will that man should communicate with nature as an intelligent and noble " master " and " guardian ", and not as a heedless " exploiter " and " destroyer ".

The development of technology and the development of contemporary civilization, which is marked by the ascendancy of technology, demand a proportional development of morals and ethics. For the present, this last development seems unfortunately to be always left behind. Accordingly, in spite of the marvel of this progress, in which it is difficult not to see also authentic signs of man's greatness, signs that in their creative seeds were revealed to us in the pages of the Book of Genesis, as early as where it describes man's creation,[11] this progress cannot fail to give rise to disquiet on many counts. The first reason for disquiet concerns the essential and fundamental question: Does this progress, which has man for its author and promoter, make human life on earth " more human " in every aspect of

[10] Cf. *Gn* 1: 28.
[11] Cf. *Gn* 1-2.

94

that life? Does it make it more "worthy of man"? There can be no doubt that in various aspects it does. But the question keeps coming back with regard to what is most essential – whether in the context of this progress man, as man, is becoming truly better, that is to say more mature spiritually, more aware of the dignity of his humanity, more responsible, more open to others, especially the neediest and the weakest, and readier to give and to aid all.

16. *Progress or threat* If therefore our time, the time of our generation, the time that is approaching the end of the second millennium of the Christian era, shows itself a time of great progress, it is also seen as a time of threat in many forms for man. The Church must speak of this threat to all people of good will and must always carry on a dialogue with them about it. Man's situation in the modern world seems indeed to be far removed from the objective demands of the moral order, from the requirements of justice, and even more of social love. We are dealing here only with that which found expression in the Creator's first message to man at the moment in which he was giving him the earth, to "subdue" it.[12] This first message was confirmed by Christ the Lord in the mystery of the Redemption. This is expressed by the Second Vatican Council in these beautiful chapters of its teaching that concern man's "kingship"; that is to say his call to share in the kingly function – the *munus regale* of Christ himself.[13] The essential meaning of this "kingship" and "dominion" of man over the visible world, which the Creator himself gave man for his task, consists in the priority of ethics over technology, in the primacy of the person over things, and in the superiority of spirit over matter.

This is why all phases of present-day progress must be followed attentively. Each stage of that progress must, so to speak, be x-rayed from this point of view. What is in question is the advancement of persons, not just the multiplying of things that people can use. It is a matter – as a contemporary philosopher has said and as the Council has stated – not so much of

[12] *Gn* 1: 28; cf. Vatican Council II, Decree on the Social Communications Media *Inter Mirifica*, 6: *AAS* 56 (1964) 147; Pastoral Constitution on the Church in the Modern World *Gaudium et Spes*, 74, 78: *AAS* 58 (1966) 1095-1096, 1101-1102.

[13] Cf. Vatican Council II, Dogmatic Constitution on the Church *Lumen Gentium*, 10, 36: *AAS* 57 (1965) 14-15, 41-42.

" having more " as of " being more ".[14] Indeed there is already a real perceptible danger that, while man's dominion over the world of things is making enormous advances, he should lose the essential threads of his dominion and in various ways let his humanity be subjected to the world and become himself something subject to manipulation in many ways – even if the manipulation is often not perceptible directly – through the whole of the organization of community life, through the production system and through pressure from the means of social communication. Man cannot relinquish himself or the place in the visible world that belongs to him; he cannot become the slave of things, the slave of economic systems, the slave of production, the slave of his own products. A civilization purely materialistic in outline condemns man to such slavery, even if at times, no doubt, this occurs contrary to the intentions and the very premises of its pioneers. The present solicitude for man certainly has at its root this problem. It is not a matter here merely of giving an abstract answer to the question: Who is man? It is a matter of the whole of the dynamism of life and civilization. It is a matter of the meaningfulness of the various initiatives of everyday life and also of the premises for many civilization programmes, political programmes, economic ones, social ones, state ones, and many others.

Text Eight

SOLLICITUDO REI SOCIALIS

Encyclical Letter of Pope John Paul II
30 December 1987
Nos. 26, 29, 30, 34, 48

26. [extract] ... Among today's positive signs we must also mention a greater realization of the limits of available resources, and of the need to respect the integrity and the cycles of nature and to take them into

---

[14] Cf. Vatican Council II, Pastoral Constitution on the Church in the Modern World *Gaudium et Spes*, 35: *AAS* 58 (1966) 1053; Pope Paul VI, *Address to Diplomatic Corps*, 7 January 1965: *AAS* 57 (1965) 232; Encyclical *Populorum Progressio*, 14: *AAS* 59 (1967) 264.

account when planning for development, rather than sacrificing them to certain demagogic ideas about the latter. Today this is called ecological concern. ...

29. [extract] ... However, in trying to achieve true development we must never lose sight of that dimension which is in the specific nature of man, who has been created by God in his image and likeness (cf. *Gn* 1: 26). It is a bodily and a spiritual nature, symbolized in the second creation account by the two elements: the earth, from which God forms man's body, and the breath of life which he breathes into man's nostrils (cf. *Gn* 2: 7).

Thus man comes to have a certain affinity with other creatures: he is called to use them, and to be involved with them. As the Genesis account says (cf. *Gn* 2: 15), he is placed in the garden with the duty of cultivating and watching over it, being superior to the other creatures placed by God under his dominion (cf. *Gn* 1: 25-26). But at the same time man must remain subject to the will of God, who imposes limits upon his use and dominion over things (cf. *Gn* 2: 16-17), just as he promises his mortality (cf. *Gn* 2: 9; *Wis* 2: 23). Thus man, being the image of God, has a true affinity with him too. On the basis of this teaching, development cannot consist only in the use, dominion over and indiscriminate possession of created things and the products of human industry, but rather in subordinating the possession, dominion and use to man's divine likeness and to his vocation to immortality. This is the transcendent reality of the human being, a reality which is seen to be shared from the beginning by a couple, a man and a woman (cf. *Gn* 1: 27), and is therefore fundamentally social.

30. According to Sacred Scripture therefore, the notion of development is not only "lay" or "profane", but it is also seen to be, while having a socio-economic dimension of its own, the modern expression of an essential dimension of man's vocation.

The fact is that man was not created, so to speak, immobile and static. The first portrayal of him, as given in the Bible, certainly presents him as a creature and image, defined in his deepest reality by the origin and affinity that constitute him. But all this plants within the human being – man and woman – the seed and the requirement of a special task to be accomplished by each individually and by them as a couple. The task is "to have dominion" over the other created beings, "to cultivate the garden". This is to be accomplished within the framework of obedience to the divine law and therefore with respect for the image received, the image which is the clear foundation of the power of dominion recognized as belonging to man as the means to his perfection (cf. *Gn* 1: 26-30; 2: 15-16; *Wis* 9: 2-3).

When man disobeys God and refuses to submit to his rule, nature rebels against him and no longer recognizes him as its "master", for he has tarnished the divine image in himself. The claim to ownership and use of created things remains still valid, but after sin its exercise becomes difficult and full of suffering (cf. *Gn* 3: 17-19).

In fact, the following chapter of Genesis shows us that the descendants of Cain build "a city", engage in sheep farming, practice the arts (music) and technical skills (metallurgy); while at the same time people began to "call upon the name of the Lord" (cf. *Gn* 4: 17-26).

The story of the human race described by Sacred Scripture is, even after the fall into sin, a story of constant achievements, which, although always called into question and threatened by sin, are nonetheless repeated, increased and extended in response to the divine vocation given from the beginning to man and to woman (cf. *Gn* 1: 26-28) and inscribed in the image which they received.

It is logical to conclude, at least on the part of those who believe in the word of God, that today's "development" is to be seen as a moment in the story which began at creation, a story which is constantly endangered by reason of infidelity to the Creator's will, and especially by the temptation to idolatry. But this "development" fundamentally corresponds to the first premises. Anyone wishing to renounce the difficult yet noble task of improving the lot of man in his totality, and of all people, with the excuse that the struggle is difficult and that constant effort is required, or simply because of the experience of defeat and the need to begin again, that person would be betraying the will of God the Creator. In this regard, in the Encyclical *Laborem Exercens* I referred to man's vocation to work, in order to emphasize the idea that it is always man who is the protagonist of development.[1]

---

[1] Cf. Encyclical Letter *Laborem Exercens* (September 14, 1981), 4: *AAS* 73 (1981), pp. 584f.; Paul VI, Encyclical Letter *Populorum Progressio*, 15: *loc. cit.*, p. 265.

Indeed, the Lord Jesus himself, in the parable of the talents, emphasizes the severe treatment given to the man who dared to hide the gift received: "You wicked slothful servant! You knew that I reap where I have not sowed and gather where I have not winnowed? ...So take the talent from him, and give it to him who has the ten talents" (*Mt* 25: 26-28). It falls to us, who receive the gifts of God in order to make them fruitful, to "sow" and "reap". If we do not, even what we have will be taken away from us.

A deeper study of these harsh words will make us commit ourselves more resolutely to the duty, which is urgent for everyone today, to work together for the full development of others: "development of the whole human being and of all people".[2]

34. Nor can the moral character of development exclude respect for the beings which constitute the natural world, which the ancient Greeks – alluding precisely to the order which distinguishes it – called the "cosmos". Such realities also demand respect, by virtue of a threefold consideration which it is useful to reflect upon carefully.

The first consideration is the appropriateness of acquiring a growing awareness of the fact that one cannot use with impunity the different categories of beings, whether living or inanimate – animals, plants, the natural elements – simply as one wishes, according to one s own economic needs. On the contrary, one must take into account the nature of each being and of its mutual connection in an ordered system, which is precisely the cosmos".

The second consideration is based on the realization – which is perhaps more urgent – that natural resources are limited; some are not, as it is said, renewable. Using them as if they were inexhaustible, with absolute dominion, seriously endangers their availability not only for the present generation but above all for generations to come.

The third consideration refers directly to the consequences of a certain type of development on the quality of life in the industrialized zones. We all know that the direct or indirect result of industrialization is, ever more frequently, the pollution of the environment, with serious consequences for the health of the population.

[2] Encyclical Letter *Populorum Progressio*, 42: *loc. cit.*, p. 278.

Once again it is evident that development, the planning which governs it, and the way in which resources are used must include respect for moral demands. One of the latter undoubtedly imposes limits on the use of the natural world. The dominion granted to man by the Creator is not an absolute power, nor can one speak of a freedom to "use and misuse", or to dispose of things as one pleases. The limitation imposed from the beginning by the Creator himself and expressed symbolically by the prohibition not to "eat of the fruit of the tree" (cf. *Gn* 2: 16-17) shows clearly enough that, when it comes to the natural world, we are subject not only to biological laws but also to moral ones, which cannot be violated with impunity.

A true concept of development cannot ignore the use of the elements of nature, the renewability of resources and the consequences of haphazard industrialization – three considerations which alert our consciences to the moral dimension of development.[3]

48. [extract] ... The Kingdom of God becomes present above all in the celebration of the sacrament of the Eucharist, which is the Lord's Sacrifice. In that celebration the fruits of the earth and the work of human hands – the bread and wine – are transformed mysteriously, but really and substantially, through the power of the Holy Spirit and the words of the minister, into the Body and Blood of the Lord Jesus Christ, the Son of God and Son of Mary, through whom the Kingdom of the Father has been made present in our midst.

The goods of this world and the work of our hands-the bread and wine-serve for the coming of the definitive Kingdom, since the Lord, through his Spirit, takes them up into himself in order to offer himself to the Father and to offer us with himself in the renewal of his one Sacrifice, which anticipates God's Kingdom and proclaims its final coming. ...

[3] Cf. *Homily at Val Visdende*, Italy (July 12, 1987), No. 5: *L'Osservatore Romano*, July 13-14, 1987; Paul VI, Apostolic Letter *Octogesima Adveniens* (May 14, 1971), 21: *AAS* 63 (1971), pp. 416f.

DOMINUM ET VIVIFICANTEM
Encyclical Letter of Pope John Paul II
18 May 1986
No. 50

50. [extract] ... "Fiat": "Be it done unto me according to your word",[1] she conceives in a virginal way a man, the Son of Man, who is the Son of God. By means of this "humanization" of the Word-Son the self-communication of God reaches its definitive fullness in the history of creation and salvation. This fullness acquires a special wealth and expressiveness in the text of John's Gospel: "The Word became flesh".[2] The Incarnation of God the Son signifies the taking up into unity with God not only of human nature, but in this human nature, in a sense, of everything that is "flesh": the whole of humanity, the entire visible and material world. The Incarnation, then, also has a cosmic significance, a cosmic dimension. The "first-born of all creation",[3] becoming incarnate in the individual humanity of Christ, unites himself in some way with the entire reality of man, which is also "flesh"[4] – and in this reality with all "flesh", with the whole of creation.

[1] *Lk* 1: 38.
[2] *Jn* 1: 14.
[3] *Col* 1: 15.
[4] Cf., for example, *Gn* 9: 11; *Deut* 5: 26; *Job* 34: 15; *Is* 40: 6; 42: 10; *Ps* 145/144: 21; *Lk* 3: 6; *1 Pet* 1: 24.

LABOREM EXERCENS
Encyclical Letter of Pope John Paul II
14 September 1981
Nos. 4, 25

4. *In the Book of Genesis.* The Church is convinced that work is a fundamental dimension of man's existence on earth. She is confirmed in this conviction by considering the whole heritage of the many sciences devoted to man: anthropology, paleontology, history, sociology, psychology and so on; they all seem to bear witness to this reality in an irrefutable way. But the source of the Church's conviction is above all the revealed word of God, and therefore what is *a conviction of the intellect* is also *a conviction of faith.* The reason is that the Church – and it is worthwhile stating it at this point – believes in man: she *thinks of man* and addresses herself to him *not only* in the light of historical experience, not only with the aid of the many methods of scientific knowledge, but in the first place in the light of the revealed word of the living God. Relating herself to man, she seeks *to express* the eternal *designs* and transcendent *destiny* which *the living God,* the Creator and Redeemer, has linked with him.

The Church finds *in the very first pages of the Book of Genesis* the source of her conviction that work is a fundamental dimension of human existence on earth. An analysis of these texts makes us aware that they express – sometimes in an archaic way of manifesting thought – the fundamental truths about man, in the context of the mystery of creation itself. These truths are decisive for man from the very beginning, and at the same time they trace out the main lines of his earthly existence, both in the state of original justice and also after the breaking, caused by sin, of the Creator's original covenant with creation in man. When man, who had been created " in the image of God . . . male and female ",[1] hears the words: " Be fruitful and *multiply, and fill the earth and subdue it* ",[2] even though these

---

[1] *Gn* 1: 27.
[2] *Gn* 1: 28.

words do not refer directly and explicitly to work, beyond any doubt they indirectly indicate it as an activity for man to carry out in the world. Indeed, they show its very deepest essence. Man is the image of God partly through the mandate received from his Creator to subdue, to dominate, the earth. In carrying out this mandate, man, every human being, reflects the very action of the Creator of the universe.

Work understood as a "transitive" activity, that is to say an activity beginning in the human subject and directed toward an external object, presupposes a specific dominion by man over "the earth", and in its turn it confirms and develops this dominion. It is clear that the term "the earth" of which the biblical text speaks is to be understood in the first place as that fragment of the visible universe that man inhabits. By extension, however, it can be understood as the whole of the visible world insofar as it comes within the range of man's influence and of his striving to satisfy his needs. The expression "subdue the earth" has an immense range. It means all the resources that the earth (and indirectly the visible world) contains and which, through the conscious activity of man, can be discovered and used for his ends. And so these words, placed at the beginning of the Bible, *never cease to be relevant.*

They embrace equally the past ages of civilization and economy, as also the whole of modern reality and future phases of development, which are perhaps already to some extent beginning to take shape, though for the most part they are still almost unknown to man and hidden from him.

While people sometimes speak of periods of "acceleration" in the economic life and civilization of humanity or of individual nations, linking these periods to the progress of science and technology and especially to discoveries which are decisive for social and economic life, at the same time it can be said that none of these phenomena of "acceleration" exceeds the essential content of what was said in that most ancient of biblical texts. As man, through his work, becomes more and more the master of the earth, and as he confirms his dominion over the visible world, again through his work, he nevertheless remains in every case and at every phase of this process within the Creator's original ordering. And this ordering remains necessarily and indissolubly linked with the fact that man was created, as male and female, "in the image of God". This *process* is, at the same time, *universal:* it embraces all human beings, every generation, every phase of economic and cultural development, and *at the same time* it is a process that takes place *within each human being,* in each conscious human subject. Each and every individual is at the same time embraced by it. Each and every individual, to the proper extent and in an incalculable number of ways, takes part in the giant process whereby man "subdues the earth" through his work.

25. *Work as a sharing in the activity of the Creator.* As the Second Vatican Council says, "throughout the course of the centuries, men have labored to better the circumstances of their lives through a monumental amount of individual and collective effort. To believers, this point is settled: considered in itself, such human activity accords with God's will. For man, created to God's image, received a mandate to subject to himself the earth and all that it contains, and to govern the world with justice and holiness; a mandate to relate himself and the totality of things to him who was to be acknowledged as the Lord and Creator of all. Thus, by the subjection of all things to man, the name of God would be wonderful in all the earth".[3]

The word of God's revelation is profoundly marked by the fundamental truth that *man, created in the image of God, shares by his work in the activity of the Creator* and that, within the limits of his own human capabilities, man in a sense continues to develop that activity, and perfects it as he advances further and further in the discovery of the resources and values contained in the whole of creation. We find this truth at the very beginning of Sacred Scripture, in the Book of Genesis, where the creation activity itself is presented in the form of "work" done by God during "six days",[4] "resting" on the seventh day.[5] Besides, the last book of Sacred Scripture echoes the same respect for what God has done through his creative "work" when it proclaims: "Great and wonderful are your deeds, O Lord God the Almighty";[6] this is similar to the Book of Genesis, which concludes the description of each day of creation with the statement: "And God saw that it was good".[7]

---

[3] Second Vatican Ecumenical Council, Pastoral Constitution on the Church in the Modern World *Gaudium et Spes,* 34: *AAS* 58 (1966), 1052-1053.

[4] Cf. *Gn* 2: 2; *Ex* 20: 8, 11; *Dt* 5: 12-14.

[5] Cf. *Gn* 2: 3.

[6] *Rev* 15: 3.

[7] *Gn* 1: 4, 10, 12, 18, 21, 25, 31.

This description of creation, which we find in the very first chapter of the Book of Genesis, is also *in a sense the first "gospel of work"*. For it shows what the dignity of work consists of: it teaches that man ought to imitate God, his Creator, in working, because man alone has the unique characteristic of likeness to God. Man ought to imitate God both in working and also in resting, since God himself wished to present his own creative activity under the form of *work and rest*. This activity by God in the world always continues, as the words of Christ attest: "My Father is working still...": [8] he works with creative power by sustaining in existence the world that he called into being from nothing, and he works with salvific power in the hearts of those whom from the beginning he has destined for "rest" [9] in union with himself in his "Father's house".[10] Therefore man's work too not only requires a rest every "seventh day",[11] but also cannot consist in the mere exercise of human strength in external action; it must leave room for man to prepare himself, by becoming more and more what in the will of God he ought to be, for the *"rest" that the Lord reserves for his servants and friends*.[12]

Awareness that man's work is a participation in God's activity ought to permeate, as the Council teaches, even *"the most ordinary everyday activities*. For, while providing the substance of life for themselves and their families, men and women are performing their activities in a way which appropriately benefits society. They can justly consider that by their labor they are unfolding the Creator's work, consulting the advantages of their brothers and sisters, and contributing by their personal industry to the realization in history of the divine plan".[13]

This Christian spirituality of work should be a heritage shared by all. Especially in the modern age, the *spirituality* of work should show the *maturity* called for by the tensions and restlessness of mind and heart. "Far from thinking that works produced by man's own talent and energy are in opposition to God's power, and that the rational creature exists as a

---

[8] *Jn* 5: 17.
[9] Cf. *Heb* 4: 1, 9-10.
[10] *Jn* 14: 2.
[11] Cf. *Dt* 5: 12-14; *Ex* 20: 8-12.
[12] Cf. *Mt* 25: 21.
[13] Second Vatican Ecumenical Council, Pastoral Constitution on the Church in the Modern World *Gaudium et Spes,* 34: AAS 58 (1966), 1052-1053.

kind of rival to the Creator, Christians are convinced that the triumphs of the human race are a sign of God's greatness and the flowering of his own mysterious design. For the greater man's power becomes, the farther his individual and community responsibility extends. ... People are not deterred by *the Christian message* from building up the world, or impelled to neglect the welfare of their fellows. They are, rather, more stringently bound to do these very things ".[14]

The knowledge that by means of work man shares in the work of creation constitutes the most profound *motive* for undertaking it in various sectors. "The faithful, therefore", we read in the Constitution *Lumen Gentium,* "must learn the deepest meaning and the value of all creation, and its orientation to the praise of God. Even by their secular activity they must assist one another to live holier lives. In this way the world will be permeated by the spirit of Christ and more effectively achieve its purpose in justice, charity and peace... Therefore, by their competence in secular fields and by their personal activity, elevated from within by the grace of Christ, let them work vigorously so that by human labor, technical skill, and civil culture created goods may be perfected according to the design of the Creator and the light of his Word ".[15]

Text Eleven

AMICI DILECTI

Apostolic Letter of Pope John Paul II
31 March 1985
No. 14

14. [extract] ... Youth should be "growth". For this purpose, contact with the visible world, with nature, is of immense importance. In one's youth this relationship to the visible world is enriching in a way that dif-

---

[14] *Ibid.*
[15] Second Vatican Ecumenical Council, Dogmatic Constitution on the Church *Lumen Gentium,* 36: *AAS* 57 (1965), 41.

fers from knowledge of the world "obtained from books". It enriches us in a direct way. One could say that by being in contact with nature we absorb into our own human existence the very mystery of creation which reveals itself to us through the untold wealth and variety of visible beings, and which at the same time is always beckoning us towards what is hidden and invisible. Wisdom-both from the inspired books[1] as also from the testimony of many brilliant minds-seems in different ways to reveal "the transparency of the world". It is good for people to read this wonderful book-the "book of nature", which lies open for each one of us. What the youthful mind and heart read in this book seems to be in perfect harmony with the exhortation to wisdom: "Acquire wisdom, acquire insight... Do not forsake her and she will keep you; love her and she will guard you".[2]

Man today, especially in the context of highly developed technical and industrial civilization, has become the explorer of nature on a grand scale, often treating it in a utilitarian way, thus destroying many of its treasures and attractions and polluting the natural environment of earthly existence. But nature is also given to us to be admired and contemplated, like a great mirror of the world. It reflects the Creator's covenant with his creature, the centre of which has been, from the beginning, in man, directly created "in the image" of the Creator.

And so my hope for you young people is that your "growth in stature and in wisdom" will come about through contact with nature. Make time for this! Do not miss it! Accept too the fatigue and effort that this contact sometimes involves, especially when we wish to attain particularly challenging goals. Such fatigue is creative, and also constitutes the element of healthy relaxation which is as necessary as study and work.

[1] Cf. e.g. *Ps* 104 [103]; *Ps* 19 [18]; *Wis* 13: 1-9; 7: 15-20.
[2] *Pr* 4: 5-7.

ADDRESS

Pope John Paul II
The United Nations Centre
Nairobi, Kenya, 18 August 1985

Ladies and Gentlemen,

1. It is always an honour for me to visit one of the Agencies of the United Nations. The ever-increasing importance of this prestigious Organization becomes more evident every year. At no time in history has there been a greater need for dialogue and collaboration at the international level and for joint efforts by nations to promote integral human development and to further justice and peace – precisely the goals to which the United Nations Organization is dedicated.

I am very grateful then for the invitation to come to this Centre today, an invitation which was extended to me by Dr Mostafa K. Tolba, the Executive director of *the United Nations Environment Programme.* In greeting him, I also greet the staff and all associated in the Agency's work. At the same time, I offer a cordial greeting to the staff of *Habitat: the United Nations Centre for Human Settlements,* also located here in Nairobi, and to its Executive Director, Dr Alcot Ramachandron.

2. For many years now, *the Catholic Church* has taken an *active interest in questions concerning the environment.* A Delegation of the Holy See participated in the Conference on the Environment held in Stockholm in 1972, the meeting which prepared the way for the establishment of the United Nations Environment Programme. My predecessor, Pope Paul VI, sent a message to the Stockholm Conference, in which he said: "We would like to tell you and all the participants of the interest with which we follow this great enterprise. The care of preserving and improving the natural environment, like the noble ambition of stimulating a first gesture of world cooperation in favour of this good necessary for everyone, meets needs that are deeply felt among the people of our times".

The Church's commitment to the conservation and improvement of our environment is linked to a command of God. In the very first pages of the Bible, we read how God created all things and then entrusted them to the care of human beings who were themselves created in his image. God said to Adam and Eve: " Be fruitful and multiply, and fill the earth and subdue it; and *have dominion* over the fish of the sea and over the birds of the air and *over every living thing* that moves upon the earth ".[1]

It is a requirement of our human dignity, and therefore a serious responsibility, to exercise dominion over creation in such a way that it truly serves the human family. Exploitation of the riches of nature must take place according to criteria that take into account not only the immediate needs of people but also the needs of future generations. In this way, the stewardship over nature, entrusted by God to man, will not be guided by short sightedness or selfish pursuit; rather, it will take into account the fact that all created goods are directed to the good of all humanity. The use of natural resources must aim at serving the integral development of present and future generations. Progress in the field of ecology, and growing awareness of the need to protect and conserve certain non-renewable natural resources, are in keeping with the demands of true stewardship. God *is glorified when creation serves the integral development of the whole human family.*

3. With the rapid acceleration of science and technology in recent decades, the environment has been subjected to far greater changes than ever before. As a result, we are offered *many new opportunities for development* and human progress; we are now able to transform our surroundings greatly, even dramatically, for the enhancement of the quality of life. On the other hand, this new ability, unless it is used with wisdom and vision, can cause tremendous and even irreparable harm in the ecological and social spheres. *The capacity for improving the environment* and *the capacity for destroying it* increase enormously each year.

The ultimate determining factor is the human person. It is not science and technology, or the increasing means of economic and material development, but the human person, and especially groups of persons, commu-

[1] *Gn* 1: 28.

nities and nations, *freely choosing* to face the problems together, who will, under God, determine the future. That is why whatever impedes human freedom or dishonours it, such as the evil of apartheid and all forms of prejudice and discrimination, is an affront to man's vocation to shape his own destiny. Eventually it will have repercussions in all areas requiring human freedom and as such can become a major stumbling block to the improvement of the environment and all of society.

Threats to the environment today are numerous: deforestation, water and air pollution, soil erosion, desertification, acid rain and many more. Ecological problems are especially acute in the tropical regions of the world, and in particular here in Africa. Nearly all the nations affected by these problems are developing nations which are, with great difficulty, undergoing various stages of industrialization. A severe shortage of energy and natural resources impedes progress and results in harsh living conditions. And the problems are often complicated by the tropical environment which makes people especially susceptible to serious endemic diseases.

Since every country has its own particular set of problems and varying amounts of natural resources, it is easy to see the difference between the problems faced by *developing nations* and those of *developed nations.* While modern industry and technology offer great hope of advancement, steps must be taken to ensure that the economic material and social development which are so important include proper consideration of the impact on the environment, both immediate and in the future.

4. The Catholic Church approaches the care and protection of the environment from the point of view of *the human person.* It is our conviction, therefore, that all ecological programmes must respect the *full dignity and freedom* of whoever might be affected by such programmes. Environment problems should be seen in relation to the needs of actual men and women, their families, their values, their unique social and cultural heritage. For the ultimate purpose of environment programmes is to enhance the quality of human life, *to place creation in the fullest way possible at the service of the human family.*

5. Perhaps nowhere do we see more clearly the *interrelatedness of the world* today than in questions concerning the environment. The growing

interdependence between individuals and between nations is keenly felt when it is a question of facing natural disasters such as droughts, typhoons, floods and earthquakes. The consequences of these stretch far beyond the regions directly affected. And the vastness and complexity of many ecological problems demand not only a combined response at local and national levels but also *substantial assistance and coordination from the international community*. As Pope Paul VI wrote to the Stockholm Conference: "Interdependence must now be met by joint responsibility; common destiny by solidarity". One could hardly overstate the international character of ecological problems or the international benefits of their solution.

These problems often require the expertise and assistance of scientists and technicians from industrialized countries. Yet the latter cannot solve them without the cooperation at every step of scientists and technicians from the countries being helped. The *transfer of technological skills* to developing countries cannot be expected to have lasting results if training is not provided for technicians and scientists from these countries themselves. The *training of local personnel* makes it possible to adapt technology in a way that fully respects the cultural and social fabric of the local communities. Local experts possess the necessary bonds with their own people to ensure a balanced sensitivity to local values and needs. They can evaluate the continuing validity of the newly transferred skills. Only when this trained personnel finally exists locally can one speak of full collaboration between countries.

6. I would now like to say a few words to those engaged in the work of the *United Nations Centre for Human Settlements,* and to all who are trying to improve the living conditions of the poor and provide shelter for the homeless. This work is of course closely related to the ecological problems of which I have been speaking. In fact it is at its very heart. As Pope Paul VI stated in his message to the United Nations Conference on Human Settlements in Vancouver in 1976: "The home, that is to say, the centre of warmth in which the family is united and the children grow in love, must remain the first concern of every programme relative to the human environment".[2] For this reason, the

---

[2] Paul VI, *Epistula ad Exc.mum Virum Berney Danson Canadensem Administrum pro Urbanis Negoffis eundemque Praesidem Conferentiae Unitarum Nationum in urbe Vancuve-*

Church's primary concern for the human person in problems of the environment includes the problems of housing and shelter as well.

Those who believe in Jesus Christ cannot forget his words: "Foxes have holes, and birds of the air have nests; but the Son of man has nowhere to lay his head ".[3] Thus *we see in the faces of the homeless the face of Christ the Lord*. And we feel impelled, by love of him and by his example of generous self-giving, to seek to do everything we can to help those living in conditions unworthy of their human dignity. At the same time, we gladly join hands with all people of good will in the worthy efforts being made to provide adequate housing for the millions of people in today's world living in absolute destitution. Nor can we remain passive or indifferent as the rapid increase of *urbanization and industrialization* creates complex problems of housing and the environment. I assure you then of the Church's great interest in and support for your commendable endeavours to provide housing for the homeless and to safeguard the human dimension of all settlements of people.

7. Five years ago, on the occasion of my first Pastoral Visit to Africa, I went to Ouagadougou *in the heart of the Sahel region* and there launched *a solemn appeal* on behalf of all those suffering from the devastating drought. In the wake of that appeal there was a most generous response, so generous in fact that it became possible to set up a special programme to assist the suffering in a more formal way. Thus, the John Paul II Foundation for the Sahel was officially begun in February 1984. This Foundation is a sign of the Church's love for the men, women and children who have been stricken by this continuing tragedy. Even though the project seems small and inadequate in the face of such vast needs, nonetheless it is a concrete effort to help the people there and to contribute in some degree to the future of the African continent, a future which ultimately rests in the hands of the African peoples themselves.

I wish to take this opportunity to renew my solemn appeal on behalf of the people of the Sahel and of other critical regions where the drought is still continuing and there is a clear *need for international assistance and solidar-*

rio *instructae ad dignas hominum lovendas habitationes, 24 May 1976: Insegnamenti di Paolo VI*, XIV (1976) 401 ff.
   [3] *Mt* 8: 20.

ity in order to provide food, drink and shelter and to solve the conflicts which are hindering efforts to help. Thus I repeat what I said in Ouagadougou five years ago: "I cannot be silent when my brothers and sisters are threatened. I become here the voice of those who have no voice, the voice of the innocent, who died because they lacked water and bread; the voice of fathers and mothers who saw their children die without understanding, or who will always see in their children the after-effects of the hunger they have suffered; the voice of the generations to come, who must -no longer live with this terrible threat weighing upon their lives. I launch an appeal to everyone! Let us not wait until the drought returns, terrible and devastating! Let us not wait for the sand to bring death again! Let us not allow the future of these peoples to remain jeopardized for ever"![4] The solidarity shown in the past has proved, by its extent and effectiveness, that it is possible to make a difference. Let our response now be even more generous and effective.

Two kinds of assistance are needed: assistance which meets the *immediate needs* of food and shelter, and assistance which will make it possible for the people now suffering to resume responsibility for their own lives, to reclaim their land and to make it once more capable of providing a stable, healthy way of life. Such *long-range programmes* make it possible for people to regain hope for the future and a feeling of dignity and self-worth.

8. Ladies and Gentlemen, as I speak to you today, I am reminded of the words of Paul VI which have become so well known: "Development is the new name for peace".[5] Yes, indeed, *integral development is a condition for peace,* and environment programmes for food and housing are *concrete ways of promoting peace.* All who serve the basic needs of their neighbours contribute building blocks to the great edifice of peace.

Peace is built slowly through good will, trust and persevering effort. It is built by international agencies and by governmental and non-governmental organizations when they engage *in common efforts to provide food and shelter* for the needy, and when they work together *to improve the environment.*

---

[4] John Paul II, *Vehemens incitamentum ad homines aquarum penuria afflictos sublevandos, in urbe Uagaduguensi ante cathedrale templum elatum, 7,* 10 May 1980: *Insegnamenti di Giovanni Paolo II,* 111, 1 (1980) 1295.

[5] Paul VI, *Populorum Progressio,* 87.

Peace is built by Heads of States and politicians when they rise above divisive ideologies and cooperate in joint efforts free of prejudice, discrimination, hatred and revenge. *Peace is the fruit of reconciliation,* and the peace of Africa depends also on the reconciliation of people in each individual country. It requires the solidarity of all Africans as brothers and sisters at the service of the whole African family and at the service of the integral development of all mankind.

Peace is built up when national budgets are finally diverted from the creation of more powerful and deadlier weapons to provide food and raw materials to meet basic human needs. And peace is consolidated with each passing year as the *use* of nuclear weapons becomes a fading memory in the conscience of humanity. And today we thank God again that forty years have passed without the use of those weapons that devastated human life, together with its environment and shelter, in Hiroshima and Nagasaki-forty years of hope and determination, forty years in a new era for humanity.

Peace is built by the men and women of *the mass media* when they bring to the attention of the public the facts about those who suffer, about refugees and the dispossessed, when they stir up in others a determination and generosity to respond to all those in need. Yes, *"development" and "a new heart" are new names for peace.* And those who make peace and promote conditions for peace shall forever be called children of God!

Text Thirteen

MESSAGE FOR THE 1990 WORLD DAY OF PEACE
Pope John Paul II
8 December 1989

Peace with God the Creator, Peace with All of Creation

Introduction

1. In our day, there is a growing awareness that world peace is threatened not only by the arms race, regional conflicts and continued injustices

among peoples and nations, but also by a lack of *due respect for nature*, by the plundering of natural resources and by a progressive decline in the quality of life. The sense of precariousness and insecurity that such a situation engenders is a seedbed for collective selfishness, disregard for others and dishonesty.

Faced with the widespread destruction of the environment, people everywhere are coming to understand that we cannot continue to use the goods of the earth as we have in the past. The public in general as well as political leaders are concerned about this problem, and experts from a wide range of disciplines are studying its causes. Moreover, a new *ecological awareness* is beginning to emerge which, rather than being downplayed, ought to be encouraged to develop into concrete programmes and initiatives.

2. Many ethical values, fundamental to the development of a *peaceful society*, are particularly relevant to the ecological question. The fact that many challenges facing the world today are interdependent confirms the need for carefully coordinated solutions based on a morally coherent world view.

For Christians, such a world view is grounded in religious convictions drawn from Revelation. That is why I should like to begin this Message with a reflection on the biblical account of creation. I would hope that even those who do not share these same beliefs will find in these pages a common ground for reflection and action.

I. *"And God saw that it was good"*

3. In the Book of Genesis, where we find God's first self-revelation to humanity (*Gn* 1-3), there is a recurring refrain: *"And God saw that it was good"*. After creating the heavens, the sea, the earth and all it contains, God created man and woman. At this point the refrain changes markedly: "And God saw everything that he had made, and behold, *it was very good* (*Gn* 1: 31). God entrusted the whole of creation to the man and woman, and only then – as we read – could he rest "from all his work" (*Gn* 2: 3).

Adam and Eve's call to share in the unfolding of God's plan of creation brought into play those abilities and gifts which distinguish the human being from all other creatures. At the same time, their call established a fixed relationship between mankind and the rest of creation. Made in the image and likeness of God, Adam and Eve were to have exercised their dominion over the earth (*Gn* 1: 28) with wisdom and love. Instead, they destroyed the existing harmony *by deliberately going against the Creator's plan*, that is, by choosing to sin. This resulted not only in man's alienation from himself, in death and fratricide, but also in the earth's "rebellion" against him (cf. *Gn* 3: 17-19; 4: 12). All of creation became subject to futility, waiting in a mysterious way to be set free and to obtain a glorious liberty together with all the children of God (cf. *Rm* 8: 20-21).

4. Christians believe that the Death and Resurrection of Christ accomplished the work of reconciling humanity to the Father, who " was pleased ... through (Christ) to reconcile to himself *all things*, whether on earth or in heaven, making peace by the blood of his cross " (*Col* 1: 19-20). Creation was thus made new (cf. *Rev* 21: 5). Once subjected to the bondage of sin and decay (cf. *Rm* 8: 21), it has now received new life while "we wait for new heavens and a new earth in which righteousness dwells " (*2 Pt* 3: 13). Thus, the Father "has made known to us in all wisdom and insight the mystery... which he set forth in Christ as a plan for the fulness of time, to unite *all things* in him, all things in heaven and things on earth " (*Eph* 1: 9-10).

5. These biblical considerations help us to understand better *the relationship between human activity and the whole of creation*. When man turns his back on the Creator's plan, he provokes a disorder which has inevitable repercussions on the rest of the created order. If man is not at peace with God, then earth itself cannot be at peace: "Therefore the land mourns and all who dwell in it languish, and also the beasts of the field and the birds of the air and even the fish of the sea are taken away " (*Hos* 4: 3).

The profound sense that the earth is "suffering" is also shared by those who do not profess our faith in God. Indeed, the increasing devastation of the world of nature is apparent to all. It results from the behaviour of people who show a callous disregard for the hidden, yet perceivable requirements of the order and harmony which govern nature itself .

People are asking anxiously if it is still possible to remedy the damage which has been done. Clearly, an adequate solution cannot be found merely in a better management or a more rational use of the earth's resources, as important as these may be. Rather, we must go to the source of the problem and face in its entirety that profound moral crisis *of which the destruction of the environment is only one troubling aspect.*

II. *The ecological crisis: a moral problem*

6. Certain elements of today's ecological crisis reveal its moral character. First among these is the *indiscriminate* application of advances in science and technology. Many recent discoveries have brought undeniable benefits to humanity. Indeed, they demonstrate the nobility of the human vocation to participate *responsibly* in God's creative action in the world. Unfortunately, it is now clear that the application of these discoveries in the fields of industry and agriculture have produced harmful long-term effects. This has led to the painful realization that *we cannot interfere in one area of the ecosystem without paying due attention both to the consequences of such interference in other areas and to the well-being of future generations.*

The gradual depletion of the ozone layer and the related "greenhouse effect" have now reached crisis proportions as a consequence of industrial growth, massive urban concentrations and vastly increased energy needs. Industrial waste, the burning of fossil fuels, unrestricted deforestation, the use of certain types of herbicides, coolants and propellants: all of these are known to harm the atmosphere and environment. The resulting meteorological and atmospheric changes range from damage to health to the possible future submersion of low-lying lands.

While in some cases the damage already done may well be irreversible, in many other cases it can still be halted. It is necessary, however, that the entire human community – individuals, States and international bodies – take seriously the responsibility that is theirs.

7. The most profound and serious indication of the moral implications underlying the ecological problem is the lack of *respect for life* evident in many of the patterns of environmental pollution. Often, the interests of production prevail over concern for the dignity of workers, while economic interests take priority over the good of individuals and even entire peoples. In these cases, pollution or environmental destruction is the result of an unnatural and reductionist vision which at times leads to a genuine contempt for man.

On another level, delicate ecological balances are upset by the uncontrolled destruction of animal and plant life or by a reckless exploitation of natural resources. It should be pointed out that all of this, even if carried out in the name of progress and well-being, is ultimately to mankind's disadvantage.

Finally, we can only look with deep concern at the enormous possibilities of biological research. We are not yet in a position to assess the biological disturbance that could result from indiscriminate genetic manipulation and from the unscrupulous development of new forms of plant and animal life, to say nothing of unacceptable experimentation regarding the origins of human life itself. It is evident to all that in any area as delicate as this, indifference to fundamental ethical norms, or their rejection, would lead mankind to the very threshold of self-destruction.

Respect for life, and above all for the dignity of the human person, is the ultimate guiding norm for any sound economic, industrial or scientific progress.

The complexity of the ecological question is evident to all. There are, however, certain underlying principles, which, while respecting the legitimate autonomy and the specific competence of those involved, can direct research towards adequate and lasting solutions. These principles are essential to the building of a peaceful society; *no peaceful society can afford to neglect either respect for life or the fact that there is an integrity to creation.*

III. *In search of a solution*

8. Theology, philosophy and science all speak of a harmonious universe, of a "cosmos" endowed with its own integrity, its own internal, dynamic balance. *This order must be respected.* The human race is called to explore this order, to examine it with due care and to make use of it while safeguarding its integrity.

On the other hand, the earth is ultimately *a common heritage, the fruits of which are for the benefit of all.* In the words of the Second Vatican Council, "God destined the earth and all it contains for the use of every individual and all peoples" (*Gaudium et Spes*, 69). This has direct consequences for the problem at hand. It is manifestly unjust that a privileged few should continue to accumulate excess goods, squandering available resources, while masses of people are living in conditions of misery at the very lowest level of subsistence. Today, the dramatic threat of ecological breakdown is teaching us the extent to which greed and selfishness – both individual and collective – are contrary to the order of creation, an order which is characterized by mutual interdependence.

9. The concepts of an ordered universe and a common heritage both point to the necessity of a *more internationally coordinated approach to the management of the earth's goods*. In many cases the effects of ecological problems transcend the borders of individual States; hence their solution cannot be found solely on the national level. Recently there have been some promising steps towards such international action, yet the existing mechanisms and bodies are clearly not adequate for the development of a comprehensive plan of action. Political obstacles, forms of exaggerated nationalism and economic interests – to mention only a few factors – impede international cooperation and long-term effective action.

The need for joint action on the international level *does not lessen the responsibility of each individual State*. Not only should each State join with others in implementing internationally accepted standards, but it should also make or facilitate necessary socio-economic adjustments within its own borders, giving special attention to the most vulnerable sectors of society. The State should also actively endeavour within its own territory to prevent destruction of the atmosphere and biosphere, by carefully monitoring , among other things, the impact of new technological or scientific advances. The State also has the responsibility of ensuring that its citizens are not exposed to dangerous pollutants or toxic wastes. *The right to a safe environment* is ever more insistently presented today as a right that must be included in an updated Charter of Human Rights.

IV. *The urgent need for a new solidarity*

10. The ecological crisis reveals the *urgent moral need for a new solidarity*, especially in relations between the developing nations and those that are highly industrialized. States must increasingly share responsibility, in complimentary ways, for the promotion of a natural and social environment that is both peaceful and healthy. The newly industrialized States cannot, for example, be asked to apply restrictive environmental standards

119

to their emerging industries unless the industrialized States first apply them within their own boundaries. At the same time, countries in the process of industrialization are not morally free to repeat the errors made in the past by others, and recklessly continue to damage the environment through industrial pollutants, radical deforestation or unlimited exploitation of non-renewable resources. In this context, there is urgent need to find a solution to the treatment and disposal of toxic wastes.

No plan or organization, however, will be able to effect the necessary changes unless world leaders are truly convinced of the absolute need for this new solidarity, which is demanded of them by the ecological crisis and which is essential for peace. *This need presents new opportunities for strengthening cooperative and peaceful relations among States.*

11. It must also be said that the proper ecological balance will not be found without *directly addressing the structural forms of poverty* that exist throughout the world. Rural poverty and unjust land distribution in many countries, for example, have led.to subsistence farming and to the exhaustion of the soil. Once their land yields no more, many farmers move on to clear new land, thus accelerating uncontrolled deforestation, or they settle in urban centres which lack the infrastructure to receive them. Likewise, some heavily indebted countries are destroying their natural heritage, at the price of irreparable ecological imbalances, in order to develop new products for export. In the face of such situations it would be wrong to assign responsibility to the poor alone for the negative environmental consequences of their actions. Rather, the poor, to whom the earth is entrusted no less than to others, must be enabled to find a way out of their poverty. This will require a courageous reform of structures, as well as new ways of relating among peoples and States.

12. But there is another dangerous menace which threatens us, namely *war*. Unfortunately, modern science already has the capacity to change the environment for hostile purposes. Alterations of this kind over the long term could have unforeseeable and still more serious consequences. Despite the international agreements which prohibit chemical, bacteriological and biological warfare, the fact is that laboratory research continues to develop new offensive weapons capable of altering the balance of nature.

Today, any form of war on a global scale would lead to incalculable ecological damage. But even local or regional wars, however limited, not only destroy human life and social structures, but also damage the land, ruining crops and vegetation as well as poisoning the soil and water. The survivors of war are forced to begin a new life in very difficult environmental conditions, which in turn create situations of extreme social unrest, with further negative consequences for the environment.

13. Modern society will find no solution to the ecological problem unless it *takes a serious look at its lifestyle*. In many parts of the world society is given to instant gratification and consumerism while remaining indifferent to the damage which these cause. As I have already stated, the seriousness of the ecological issue lays bare the depth of man's moral crisis. If an appreciation of the value of the human person and of human life is lacking, we will also lose interest in others and in the earth itself. Simplicity, moderation and discipline, as well as a spirit of sacrifice, must become a part of everyday life, lest all suffer the negative consequences of the careless habits of a few.

An education in ecological responsibility is urgent: responsibility for oneself, for others, and for the earth. This education cannot be rooted in mere sentiment or empty wishes. Its purpose cannot be ideological or political. It must not be based on a rejection of the modern world or a vague desire to return to some " paradise lost ". Instead, a true education in responsibility entails a genuine conversion in ways of thought and behaviour. Churches and religious bodies, non-governmental and governmental organizations, indeed all members of society, have a precise role to play in such education. The first educator, however, is the family, where the child learns to respect his neighbour and to love nature.

14. *Finally, the aesthetic value of creation cannot be overlooked.* Our very contact with nature has a deep restorative power; contemplation of its magnificence imparts peace and serenity. The Bible speaks again and again of the goodness and beauty of creation, which is called to glorify God (cf. *Gn* 1: 4ff.; *Ps* 8: 2; 104: 1ff.; *Wis* 13: 3-5; *Sir* 39: 16, 33; 43: 1, 9). More difficult perhaps, but no less profound, is the contemplation of the works of human ingenuity. Even cities can have a beauty all their own, one that ought to motivate people to care for their surroundings. Good

urban planning is an important part of environmental protection, and respect for the natural contours of the land is an indispensable prerequisite for ecologically sound development. The relationship between a good aesthetic education and the maintenance of a healthy environment cannot be overlooked.

V. *The ecological crisis: a common responsibility*

15. Today the ecological crisis has assumed such proportions as to be *the responsibility of everyone*. As I have pointed out, its various aspects demonstrate the need for concerted efforts aimed at establishing the duties and obligations that belong to individuals, peoples, States and the international community. This not only goes hand in hand with efforts to build true peace, but also confirms and reinforces those efforts in a concrete way. When the ecological crisis is set within the broader context of *the search for peace* within society, we can understand better the importance of giving attention to what the earth and its atmosphere are telling us: namely, that there is an order in the universe which must be respected, and that the human person, endowed with the capability of choosing freely, has a grave responsibility to preserve this order for the well-being of future generations. I wish to repeat that *the ecological crisis is a moral issue*.

Even men and women without any particular religious conviction, but with an acute sense of their responsibilities for the common good, recognize their obligation to contribute to the restoration of a healthy environment. All the more should men and women who believe in God the Creator, and who are thus convinced that there is a well-defined unity and order in the world, feel called to address the problem. Christians, in particular, realize that their responsibility within creation and their duty towards nature and the Creator are an essential part of their faith. As a result, they are conscious of a vast field of ecumenical and interreligious cooperation opening up before them.

16. At the conclusion of this Message, I should like to address directly my brothers and sisters in the Catholic Church, in order to remind them of their serious obligation to care for all of creation. The commitment of believers to a healthy environment for everyone stems directly from their belief in God the Creator, from their recognition of the effects of original

and personal sin, and from the certainty of having been redeemed by Christ. Respect for life and for the dignity of the human person extends also to the rest of creation, which is called to join man in praising God (cf. *Ps* 148: 96).

In 1979, I proclaimed Saint Francis of Assisi as the heavenly Patron of those who promote ecology (cf. Apostolic Letter *Inter Sanctos*: *AAS* 71 [1979], 1509f.). He offers Christians an example of genuine and deep respect for the integrity of creation. As a friend of the poor who was loved by God's creatures, Saint Francis invited all of creation – animals, plants, natural forces, even Brother Sun and Sister Moon – to give honour and praise to the Lord. The poor man of Assisi gives us striking witness that when we are at peace with God we are better able to devote ourselves to building up that peace with all creation which is inseparable from peace among all peoples.

It is my hope that the inspiration of Saint Francis will help us to keep ever alive a sense of " fraternity " with all those good and beautiful things which Almighty God has created. And may he remind us of our serious obligation to respect and watch over them with care, in light of that greater and higher fraternity that exists within the human family.

Text Fourteen

CENTESIMUS ANNUS
Encyclical Letter of Pope John Paul II
30 December 1987
Nos. 37, 38, 40, 52

37. Equally worrying is *the ecological question* which accompanies the problem of consumerism and which is closely connected to it. In his desire to have and to enjoy rather than to be and to grow, man consumes the resources of the earth and his own life in an excessive and disordered way. At the root of the senseless destruction of the natural environment lies an anthropological error, which unfortunately is widespread in our

day. Man, who discovers his capacity to transform and in a certain sense create the world through his own work, forgets that this is always based on God's prior and original gift of the things that are. Man thinks that he can make arbitrary use of the earth, subjecting it without restraint to his will, as though it did not have its own requisites and a prior God-given purpose, which man can indeed develop but must not betray. Instead of carrying out his role as a co-operator with God in the work of creation, man sets himself up in place of God and thus ends up provoking a rebellion on the part of nature, which is more tyrannized than governed by him.[1]

In all this, one notes first the poverty or narrowness of man's outlook, motivated as he is by a desire to possess things rather than to relate them to the truth, and lacking that disinterested, unselfish and aesthetic attitude that is born of wonder in the presence of being and of the beauty which enables one to see in visible things the message of the invisible God who created them. In this regard, humanity today must be conscious of its duties and obligations towards future generations.

38. In addition to the irrational destruction of the natural environment, we must also mention the more serious destruction of the *human environment,* something which is by no means receiving the attention it deserves. Although people are rightly worried — though much less than they should be — about preserving the natural habitats of the various animal species threatened with extinction, because they realize that each of these species makes its particular contribution to the balance of nature in general, too little effort is made to *safeguard the moral conditions for an authentic "human ecology".* Not only has God given the earth to man, who must use it with respect for the original good purpose for which it was given to him, but man too is God's gift to man. He must therefore respect the natural and moral structure with which he has been endowed. In this context, mention should be made of the serious problems of modern urbanization, of the need for urban planning which is concerned with how people are to live, and of the attention which should be given to a "social ecology" of work.

---

[1] Cf. Encyclical Letter *Sollicitudo Rei Socialis,* 34: *loc. cit.,* 559f.; Message for the 1990 World Day of Peace: *AAS* 82 (1990), 147-156.

Man receives from God his essential dignity and with it the capacity to transcend every social order so as to move towards truth and goodness. But he is also conditioned by the social structure in which he lives, by the education he has received and by his environment. These elements can either help or hinder his living in accordance with the truth. The decisions which create a human environment can give rise to specific structures of sin which impede the full realization of those who are in any way oppressed by them. To destroy such structures and replace them with more authentic forms of living in community is a task which demands courage and patience.[2]

40. It is the task of the State to provide for the defence and preservation of common goods such as the natural and human environments, which cannot be safeguarded simply by market forces. Just as in the time of primitive capitalism the State had the duty of defending the basic rights of workers, so now, with the new capitalism, the State and all of society have the duty of *defending those collective goods* which, among others, constitute the essential framework for the legitimate pursuit of personal goals on the part of each individual.

Here we find a new limit on the market: there are collective and qualitative needs which cannot be satisfied by market mechanisms. There are important human needs which escape its logic. There are goods which by their very nature cannot and must not be bought or sold. Certainly the mechanisms of the market offer secure advantages: they help to utilize resources better; they promote the exchange of products; above all they give central place to the person's desires and preferences, which, in a contract, meet the desires and preferences of another person. Nevertheless, these mechanisms carry the risk of an "idolatry" of the market, an idolatry which ignores the existence of goods which by their nature are not and cannot be mere commodities.

52. Pope Benedict XV and his Successors clearly understood this danger.[3] I myself, on the occasion of the recent tragic war in the Persian

---

[2] Cf. Apostolic Exhortation *Reconciliatio et Poenitentia* (December 2, 1984), 16: *AAS* 77 (1985), 213-217; Pius XI, Encyclical Letter *Quadragesimo Anno*, III: *loc. cit.*, 219.

[3] Cf. Benedict XV, Exhortation *Ubi Primum* (September 8, 1914): *AAS* 6 (1914), 501f.; Pius XI, Radio Message to the Catholic Faithful and to the entire world (September 29, 1938): *AAS* 30 (1938), 309f.; Pius XII, Radio Message to the entire world (August 24,

Gulf, repeated the cry: "Never again war!". No, never again war, which destroys the lives of innocent people, teaches how to kill, throws into upheaval even the lives of those who do the killing and leaves behind a trail of resentment and hatred, thus making it all the more difficult to find a just solution of the very problems which provoked the war. Just as the time has finally come when in individual States a system of private vendetta and reprisal has given way to the rule of law, so too a similar step forward is now urgently needed in the international community. Furthermore, it must not be forgotten that at the root of war there are usually real and serious grievances: injustices suffered, legitimate aspirations frustrated, poverty, and the exploitation of multitudes of desperate people who see no real possibility of improving their lot by peaceful means.

For this reason, another name for peace is *development*.[4] Just as there is a collective responsibility for avoiding war, so too there is a collective responsibility for promoting development. Just as within individual societies it is possible and right to organize a solid economy which will direct the functioning of the market to the common good, so too there is a similar need for adequate interventions on the international level. For this to happen, *a great effort must be made to enhance mutual understanding and knowledge, and to increase the sensitivity of consciences.* This is the culture which is hoped for, one which fosters trust in the human potential of the poor, and consequently in their ability to improve their condition through work or to make a positive contribution to economic prosperity. But to accomplish this, the poor — be they individuals or nations — need to be provided with realistic opportunities. Creating such conditions calls for a *concerted worldwide effort to promote development,* an effort which also involves sacrificing the positions of income and of power enjoyed by the more developed economies.[5]

This may mean making important changes in established life-styles, in order to limit the waste of environmental and human resources, thus

1939): *AAS* 31 (1939), 333-335; John XXIII, Encyclical Letter *Pacem in Terris*, III: *loc. cit.*, 285-289; Paul VI, Discourse at the United Nations (October 4, 1965): *AAS* 57 (1965), 877-885.

   [4] Cf. Paul VI, Encyclical Letter *Populorum Progressio*, 76-77: *loc. cit.*, 294f.
   [5] Cf. Apostolic Exhortation *Familiaris Consortio*, 48: *loc. cit.*, 139f.

enabling every individual and all the peoples of the earth to have a sufficient share of those resources. In addition, the new material and spiritual resources must be utilized which are the result of the work and culture of peoples who today are on the margins of the international community, so as to obtain an overall human enrichment of the family of nations

Text Fifteen

EVANGELIUM VITAE
Encyclical Letter of Pope John Paul II
25 March 1995
Nos. 27, 42

27. [extract] ... Another welcome sign is the growing attention being paid to the *quality of life* and to *ecology,* especially in more developed societies, where people's expectations are no longer concentrated so much on problems of survival as on the search for an overall improvement of living conditions. Especially significant is the reawakening of an ethical reflection on issues affecting life. The emergence and ever more widespread development of *bioethics* is promoting more reflection and dialogue – between believers and non-believers, as well as between followers of different religions – on ethical problems, including fundamental issues pertaining to human life.

42. To defend and promote life, to show reverence and love for it, is a task which God entrusts to every man, calling him as his living image to share in his own lordship over the world: "God blessed them, and God said to them, 'Be fruitful and multiply, and fill the earth and subdue it; and have dominion over the fish of the sea and over the birds of the air and over every living thing that moves upon the earth'" (*Gn* 1: 28).

The biblical text clearly shows the breadth and depth of the lordship which God bestows on man. It is a matter first of all of *dominion over the earth and over every living creature,* as the Book of Wisdom makes clear: "O God of my fathers and Lord of mercy... by your wisdom you have formed man, to have dominion over the creatures you have made, and rule the world in holiness and righteousness" (*Wis* 9: 1, 2-3). The Psalmist too extols the dominion given to man as a sign of glory and honour from his Creator: "You have given him dominion over the works of your hands; you have put all things under his feet, all sheep and oxen, and also the beasts of the field, the birds of the air, and the fish of the sea, whatever passes along the paths of the sea" (*Ps* 8: 6-8).

As one called to till and look after the garden of the world (cf. *Gn* 2: 15), man has a specific responsibility towards *the environment in which he lives,* towards the creation which God has put at the service of his personal dignity, of his life, not only for the present but also for future generations. It is the *ecological question* – ranging from the preservation of the natural habitats of the different species of animals and of other forms of life to "human ecology" properly speaking[1] – which finds in the Bible clear and strong ethical direction, leading to a solution which respects the great good of life, of every life. In fact, "the dominion granted to man by the Creator is not an absolute power, nor can one speak of a freedom to 'use and misuse', or to dispose of things as one pleases. The limitation imposed from the beginning by the Creator himself and expressed symbolically by the prohibition not to 'eat of the fruit of the tree' (cf. *Gn* 2: 16-17) shows clearly enough that, when it comes to the natural world, we are subject not only to biological laws but also to moral ones, which cannot be violated with impunity".[2]

---

[1] Cf. John Paul II, Encyclical Letter *Centesimus Annus* (1 May 1991), 38: *AAS* 83 (1991), 840-841.

[2] John Paul II, Encyclical Letter *Sollicitudo Rei Socialis* (30 December 1987), 34: *AAS* 80 (1988), 560.

Text Sixteen

FIDES ET RATIO
Encyclical Letter of Pope John Paul II
14 September 1998
Nos. 98, 104

98. [extract] ... Throughout the Encyclical I underscored clearly the fundamental role of truth in the moral field. In the case of the more pressing ethical problems, this truth demands of moral theology a careful enquiry rooted unambiguously in the word of God. In order to fulfil its mission, moral theology must turn to a philosophical ethics which looks to the truth of the good, to an ethics which is neither subjectivist nor utilitarian. Such an ethics implies and presupposes a philosophical anthropology and a metaphysics of the good. Drawing on this organic vision, linked necessarily to Christian holiness and to the practice of the human and supernatural virtues, moral theology will be able to tackle the various problems in its competence, such as peace, social justice, the family, the defence of life and the natural environment, in a more appropriate and effective way.

104. Philosophical thought is often the only ground for understanding and dialogue with those who do not share our faith. The current ferment in philosophy demands of believing philosophers an attentive and competent commitment, able to discern the expectations, the points of openness and the key issues of this historical moment. Reflecting in the light of reason and in keeping with its rules, and guided always by the deeper understanding given them by the word of God, Christian philosophers can develop a reflection which will be both comprehensible and appealing to those who do not yet grasp the full truth which divine Revelation declares. Such a ground for understanding and dialogue is all the more vital nowadays, since the most pressing issues facing humanity – ecology, peace and the co-existence of different races and cultures, for instance – may possibly find a solution if there is a clear and honest collaboration between Christians and the followers of other religions and all those who, while not sharing a religious belief, have at heart the renewal of humanity. The Sec-

ond Vatican Council said as much: "For our part, the desire for such dialogue, undertaken solely out of love for the truth and with all due prudence, excludes no one, neither those who cultivate the values of the human spirit while not yet acknowledging their Source, nor those who are hostile to the Church and persecute her in various ways".[1] A philosophy in which there shines even a glimmer of the truth of Christ, the one definitive answer to humanity's problems,[2] will provide a potent underpinning for the true and planetary ethics which the world now needs.

Text Seventeen

VITA CONSECRATA

Post-Synodal Apostolic Exhortation of Pope John Paul II
25 March 1996
No. 90

90. [extract] Even before being a service on behalf of the poor, *evangelical poverty is a value in itself*, since it recalls the first of the Beatitudes in the imitation of the poor Christ. Its primary meaning, in fact, is to attest that God is the true wealth of the human heart. Precisely for this reason evangelical poverty forcefully challenges the idolatry of money, making a prophetic appeal as it were to society, which in so many parts of the developed world risks losing the sense of proportion and the very meaning of things. Thus, today more than in other ages, the call of evangelical poverty is being felt also among those who are aware of the scarcity of the planet's resources and who invoke respect for and the conservation of creation by reducing consumption, by living more simply and by placing a necessary brake on their own desires.

Consecrated persons are therefore asked to bear a renewed and vigorous evangelical witness to self-denial and restraint, in a form of fraternal

[1] Pastoral Constitution on the Church in the Modern World *Gaudium et Spes*, 92.
[2] Cf. *ibid.* No. 10.

life inspired by principles of simplicity and hospitality, also as an example to those who are indifferent to the needs of their neighbour. This witness will of course be accompanied by *a preferential love for the poor* and will be shown especially by sharing the conditions of life of the most neglected. There are many communities which live and work among the poor and the marginalized; they embrace their conditions of life and share in their sufferings, problems and perils. ...

Text Eighteen

ECCLESIA IN AMERICA

Post-Synodal Apostolic Exhortation of Pope John Paul II
22 January 1999
Nos. 20, 25

20. [extract] ... However, if globalization is ruled merrely by the laws of the market applied to suit the powerful, the consequences cannot but be negative. These are, for example, the absolutizing of the economy, unemployment, the reduction and deterioration of public services, the destruction of the environment and natural resources, the growing distance beween rich and poor, unfair cmpetition which puts the poor nations in a situation of ever increasing inferiority.[1] While acknowledging the positive values which come with globalization, the Church considers with concern the negative aspects which follow in its wake.

25. *Ecological concern.* "And God saw that it was good" (*Gn* 1: 25). These words from the first chapter of the Book of Genesis reveal the meaning of what God has done. To men and women, the crown of the entire process of creation, the Creator entrusts the care of the earth (cf. *Gn* 2: 15). This brings concrete obligations in the area of ecology for every

[1] Cf. *Popositio* 74.

person. Fulfillment of these obligations supposes an openness to a spiritual and ethical perspective capable of overcoming selfish attitudes and "life-styles which lead to the depletion of natural resources".[2]

In this area too, so relevant today, the action of believers is more important than ever. Alongside legislative and governmental bodies, all people of good will must work to ensure the effective protection of the environment, understood as a gift from God. How much ecological abuse and destruction there is in many parts of America! It is enough to think of the uncontrolled emission of harmful gases or the dramatic phenomenon of forest fires, sometimes deliberately set by people driven by selfish interest. Devastations such as these could lead to the desertification of many parts of America, with the inevitable consequences of hunger and misery. This is an especially urgent problem in the forests of Amazonia, an immense territory extending into different countries: from Brazil to Guyana, Surinam, Venezuela, Colombia, Ecuador, Peru and Bolivia.[3] This is one of the world's most precious natural regions because of its bio-diversity which makes it vital for the environmental balance of the entire planet.

Text Nineteen

ECCLESIA IN ASIA

Post-Synodal Apostolic Exhortation of Pope John Paul II
6 November 1999
No. 41

41. *The Environment.* [extract] When concern for economic and technological progress is not accompanied by concern for the balance of the ecosystem, our earth is inevitably exposed to serious environmental damage, with consequent harm to human beings. Blatant disrespect for the environment will continue as long as the earth and its potential are seen

---

[2] *Propositio* 36.
[3] Cf. *ibid.*

merely as objects of immediate use and consumption, to be manipulated by an unbridled desire for profit.[1] It is the duty of Christians and of all who look to God as the Creator to protect the environment by restoring a sense of reverence for the whole of God's creation. It is the Creator's will that man should treat nature not as a ruthless exploiter but as an intelligent and responsible administrator.[2] The Synod Fathers pleaded in a special way for greater responsibility on the part of the leaders of nations, legislators, business people and all who are directly involved in the management of the earth's resources.[3] They underlined the need to educate people, especially the young, in environmental responsibility, training them in the stewardship over creation which God has entrusted to humanity. The protection of the environment is not only a *technical* question; it is also and above all an *ethical* issue. All have a moral duty to care for the environment, not only for their own good but also for the good of future generations. ...

Text Twenty

ECCLESIA IN OCEANIA

Post-Synodal Apostolic Exhortation of Pope John Paul II

22 November 2001

No. 31

31. *The Environment.* Oceania is a part of the world of great natural beauty, and it has succeeded in preserving areas that remain unspoiled. The region still offers to indigenous peoples a place to live in harmony with nature and one another.[1] Because creation was entrusted to human stewardship, the natural world is not just a resource to be exploited but also a reality to be

[1] Cf. John Paul II, Encyclical Letter *Redemptor Hominis* (4 March 1979), 15: *AAS* 71 (1979), 287.

[2] Cf. *ibid.*

[3] Cf. *Propositio* 47.

[1] Cf. *Propositio* 19.

respected and even reverenced as a gift and trust from God. It is the task of human beings to care for, preserve and cultivate the treasures of creation. The Synod Fathers called upon the people of Oceania to rejoice always in the glory of creation in a spirit of thanksgiving to the Creator.

Yet the natural beauty of Oceania has not escaped the ravages of human exploitation. The Synod Fathers called upon the governments and peoples of Oceania to protect this precious environment for present and future generations.[2] It is their special responsibility to assume on behalf of all humanity stewardship of the Pacific Ocean, containing over one half of the earth's total supply of water. The continued health of this and other oceans is crucial for the welfare of peoples not only in Oceania but in every part of the world.

The natural resources of Oceania need to be protected against the harmful policies of some industrialized nations and increasingly powerful transnational corporations which can lead to deforestation, despoliation of the land, pollution of rivers by mining, over-fishing of profitable species, or fouling the fishing-grounds with industrial and nuclear waste. The dumping of nuclear waste in the area constitutes an added danger to the health of the indigenous population. Yet it is also important to recognize that industry can bring great benefits when undertaken with due respect for the rights and the culture of the local population and for the integrity of the environment.

Text Twenty-One

TERTIO MILLENNIO ADVENIENTE
Apostolic Letter of Pope John Paul II
10 November 1994
Nos. 13, 46

13. The prescriptions for the jubilee year largely remained ideals – more a hope than an actual fact. They thus became a *prophetia futuri* insofar as they foretold the freedom which would be won by the coming Messiah.

[2] Cf. *ibid.*

134

Even so, on the basis of the juridical norms contained in these prescriptions a kind of *social doctrine* began to emerge, which would then more clearly develop beginning with the New Testament. *The jubilee year was meant to restore equality among all the children of Israel,* offering new possibilities to families which had lost their property and even their personal freedom. On the other hand, the jubilee year was a reminder to the rich that a time would come when their Israelite slaves would once again become their equals and would be able to reclaim their rights.

At the times prescribed by Law, a jubilee year had to be proclaimed, to assist those in need. This was required by just government. *Justice, according to the Law of Israel, consisted above all in the protection of the weak,* and a king was supposed to be outstanding in this regard, as the Psalmist says: "He delivers the needy when he calls, the poor and him who has no helper. He has pity on the weak and the needy, and saves the lives of the needy" (*Ps* 72: 12-13). *The foundations of this tradition were strictly theological,* linked first of all with the theology of Creation and with that of Divine Providence. It was a common conviction, in fact, that *to God alone, as Creator, belonged the "dominium altum"* – lordship over all Creation and over the earth in particular (cf. *Lev* 25: 23). If in his Providence God had given the earth to humanity, that meant that he had given it to everyone. Therefore *the riches of Creation were to be considered as a common good of the whole of humanity.* Those who possessed these goods as personal property were really only stewards, ministers charged with working in the name of God, who remains the sole owner in the full sense, since it is God's will that created goods should serve everyone in a just way. *The jubilee year was meant to restore this social justice.* The social doctrine of the Church, which has always been a part of Church teaching and which has developed greatly in the last century, particularly after the Encyclical *Rerum Novarum,* is rooted in the tradition of the jubilee year.

46. In this *eschatological perspective,* believers should be called to a renewed appreciation of the theological virtue *of hope,* which they have already heard proclaimed "in the word of the truth, the Gospel" (*Col* 1: 5). The basic attitude of hope, on the one hand encourages the Christian not to lose sight of the final goal which gives meaning and value to life, and on the other, offers solid and profound reasons for a daily commitment to transform reality in order to make it correspond to God's plan.

As the Apostle Paul reminds us: "We know that the whole creation has been groaning in travail together until now; and not only the creation, but we ourselves, who have the first fruits of the Spirit, groan inwardly as we wait for adoption as sons, the redemption of our bodies. For in this hope we were saved" (*Rm* 8: 22-24). Christians are called to prepare for the Great Jubilee of the beginning of the Third Millennium *by renewing their hope in the definitive coming of the Kingdom of God,* preparing for it daily in their hearts, in the Christian community to which they belong, in their particular social context, and in world history itself.

There is also need for a better appreciation and understanding of *the signs of hope present in the last part of this century,* even though they often remain hidden from our eyes. *In society in general,* such signs of hope include: scientific, technological and especially medical progress in the service of human life, a greater awareness of our responsibility for the environment, efforts to restore peace and justice wherever they have been violated, a desire for reconciliation and solidarity among different peoples, particularly in the complex relationship between the North and the South of the world. *In the Church,* they include a greater attention to the voice of the Spirit through the acceptance of charisms and the promotion of the laity, a deeper commitment to the cause of Christian unity and the increased interest in dialogue with other religions and with contemporary culture.

Text Twenty-Two

INCARNATIONIS MYSTERIUM
Bull of Indiction of the Jubilee of the Year 2000
29 November 1998
No. 12

12. One sign of the mercy of God which is especially necessary today is the sign of *charity,* which opens our eyes to the needs of those who are poor and excluded. Such is the situation affecting vast sectors of society and casting its shadow of death upon whole peoples. The human race is

facing forms of slavery which are new and more subtle than those of the past; and for too many people freedom remains a word without meaning. Some nations, especially the poorer ones, are oppressed by a debt so huge that repayment is practically impossible. It is clear, therefore, that there can be no real progress without effective cooperation between the peoples of every language, race, nationality and religion. The abuses of power which result in some dominating others must stop: such abuses are sinful and unjust. Whoever is concerned to accumulate treasure only on earth (cf. *Mt* 6: 19) "is not rich in the sight of God" (*Lk* 12: 21).

There is also a need to create a new culture of international solidarity and cooperation, where all – particularly the wealthy nations and the private sector – accept responsibility for an economic model which serves everyone. There should be no more postponement of the time when the poor Lazarus can sit beside the rich man to share the same banquet and be forced no more to feed on the scraps that fall from the table (cf. *Lk* 16: 19-31). Extreme poverty is a source of violence, bitterness and scandal; and to eradicate it is to do the work of justice and therefore the work of peace.

The Jubilee is a further summons to conversion of heart through a change of life. It is a reminder to all that they should give absolute importance neither to the goods of the earth, since these are not God, nor to man's domination or claim to domination, since the earth belongs to God and to him alone: "the earth is mine and you are strangers and sojourners with me" (*Lev* 25: 23). May this year of grace touch the hearts of those who hold in their hands the fate of the world's peoples!

APPENDICES

Paper of the Holy See
to the IV Preparatory Committee Meeting for the
World Summit for Sustainable Development
Bali, Indonesia, 27 May – 7 June 2002

Introduction

1. The World Summit for Sustainable Development (WSSD), meeting 10 years after the Rio Earth Summit, provides the nations of the world with an opportunity to assess the progress made in the last decade, to reinforce the positive gains made while reducing the negative elements that still persist.

Addressing the *three pillars of sustainable development* – the economic, the social and the environmental – the WSSD endeavors to safeguard and improve the material conditions that will be passed on to future generations of all societies. This endeavor will be even more praiseworthy if it is a *true sign of human solidarity*, bridging important national, cultural, generational and other differences, on behalf of the common good, which obviously includes the preservation and cultivation of the earth's resources. To achieve this, any society must be rooted in *solid ethical values* or it is without direction and lacks the necessary foundations upon which the sought-after development can be built and sustained. These efforts are best directed in finding ways to better order human society by guaranteeing basic requirements of justice, human rights, peace and freedom. The WSSD will prove to be a worthy contribution to an improved state of the world if it can successfully balance and indeed *prioritize* its efforts to improve the living conditions of all.

Sustainable Development as a Part of Integral Human Development

2. The concept of sustainable development is taken to mean the process of meeting the needs of the present without compromising the ability of

future generations to meet their own needs. This concept has to be understood from the perspective of integral human development. The development we speak of here "cannot be limited to mere economic growth. In order to be authentic, it must be complete, integral, that is, it has to promote the good of every man and of the whole man".[1] The WSSD must take care to ensure that sustainable development efforts explicitly serve the integral development of the human person.

All institutions, especially those of an international scope, may be tempted to place their own preservation above all else and at the expense of serving those they were meant to serve. Once an institution does this, it loses its primary objective and purpose. The principle to follow is not that of allowing economic, social and political factors to prevail over the human being, but for the dignity of the human person to be put above everything else.

Recognizing Human Dignity as a Basis for Sustainable Development

3. The first principle of the Rio Declaration states: "Human beings are at the center of sustainable development concerns"; as such it is the starting point for the discussion of sustainable development and must be recognized as the basis for the work of the WSSD. It helps focus the special responsibility human beings have not only to each other but for the environment.

Following the principle of human dignity is the complete notion of *human ecology*, which rests primarily on ensuring and safeguarding moral conditions in the action of the human being in the environment. It must also be noted that the "first and fundamental structure for 'human ecology' is *the family*, in which man receives his first formative ideas about truth and goodness, and learns what it means to love and to be loved, and thus what it actually means to be a person".[2] In this context, particular attention should be given to a "social ecology" of work.[3]

---

[1] Pope Paul VI, *Populorum Progressio*, 14.
[2] Pope John Paul II, *Centesimus Annus*, 39.
[3] *Ibid*. No. 38.

Globalization, Cultural Identity and Sustainable Development

4. The setting of the WSSD is that of a globalizing world, characterized by the growing integration of economies and societies. Here, it is necessary to recall that "globalization, *a priori*, is neither good nor bad. It will be what people make of it. No system is an end in itself, and it is necessary to insist that globalization, like any other system, must be at the service of the human person; it must serve solidarity and the common good".[4]

There are concerns that globalization has also become a cultural phenomenon, where the individual has begun to doubt his own ability and aptitude to really shape the milieu in which he lives, and the things he has created. Accordingly, sustainable development must be based on a solid ethical basis that respects the diversity and importance of cultures, which are "life's interpretative keys. In particular, it must not deprive the poor of what remains most precious to them, including their religious beliefs and practices, since genuine religious convictions are the clearest manifestations of human freedom".[5]

It is also possible that greater integration brings cultures closer together, more in the form of mutual exchange rather than a clash, and often promotes greater understanding and interdependence among cultures. While the sudden intermingling of cultures may bring out social tensions and antagonisms, a more complete understanding of the role of culture in human development and a more sincere "dialogue among cultures and civilizations"[6] may help lessen these difficulties.

Important Issues for the WSSD

5. *a*) It is absolutely necessary to give priority to *poverty eradication* with respect to both human dignity and solidarity. A necessary element in affirming human dignity is to *ensure that the poor are seen as active participants* in poverty eradication efforts. There is a distinct possibility that too many of the schemes currently under discussion look at the poor sim-

---

[4] Pope John Paul II, *Address to the Pontifical Academy of Social Sciences*, 27 April 2001, No. 2.

[5] *Ibid.* No. 4.

[6] Cf. Pope John Paul II, *Message for the 2001 World Day of Peace*.

ply as a problem rather than as potentially productive and creative actors in society.[7]

5. *b*) The delivery of *employment* opportunities, *education, basic health care* and adequate *shelter* is crucial. Forms of social insurance and worker re-training that protect the vulnerable while also providing timely and efficient incentives for continual advancement are needed.

5. *c*) *New patterns of consumption and production* should be examined and promoted in accordance with the principles of human dignity and solidarity. Within the concept of *environmental stewardship*, it is the human person which exercises power, intelligence and responsibility to help order the world. This concept can be further developed by promoting systems that allow for the conservation and sustainable use of natural resources.

5. *d*) Since more than half of the world's population still lives in rural areas and the *rural poor* lack access to the most basic social services, they must be given increased attention and consideration. The rise of and priority given to modern urbanization often has been the cause for the rural populations to be forgotten. This makes their addressing of basic human needs very difficult and results in limited consideration for environmental sustainability. Rural development merits being given higher priority in sustainable development concerns.

5. *e*) *Water* is a fundamental necessity for life,. Adequate supplies of water of good quality need to be ensured for everyone. However, too many people have no access to clean drinking water and sanitation. This has tremendous negative health and development effects. Increased access to fresh water will bring more food, less starvation, better health and a general boost to sustainable development.

[7] "[W]e realize that the major economic problems of our time do not depend on a lack of resources but on the fact that present economic, social and cultural structures are ill-equipped to meet the demands of genuine development. Rightly then, the poor, both in developing countries and in the prosperous and wealthy countries, ' ask for the right to share in enjoying material goods and to make good use of their capacity to work, thus creating a world that is more just and prosperous for all. The advancement of the poor constitutes a great opportunity for the moral, cultural and even economic growth of all humanity'. Let us look at the poor not as a problem, but as people who can become the principal builders of a new and more human future for everyone" (*Message of Pope John Paul II for the 2000 World Day of Peace*, No. 14).

Solidarity: More Effective International Cooperation

6. Solidarity is a firm and persevering determination to commit oneself to the common good. Much more than vague promises of support or feelings of compassion, solidarity has a spiritual quality that must become more deeply rooted in our approach to international problems. Pope John Paul II has called for a *"globalization of solidarity"*, which ensures that globalization will not take place to the detriment of the least favored and the weakest if it is based on a complete conception of the human person, on a adequate understanding of the dignity and rights of the person.[8] To the extent that the WSSD identifies issues of global concern, especially poverty eradication, there is a need " for rethinking international cooperation in terms of a new culture of solidarity ".[9]

Efforts towards *international governance* in the area of sustainable development will help to produce a more coherent framework for development, especially if based on a common set of principles and adopt measures to ensure transparency and accountability. There is a need "for effective international agencies [to] oversee and direct the economy to the common good ... [and to] give sufficient support and consideration to peoples and countries which have little weight in the international market but which are burdened by the most acute and desperate needs ".[10] But without a clear set of priorities and a more definite plan of implementation, any agreement reached will be in danger of remaining unfulfilled. Once again, a solid ethical basis for sustainable development will help clarify the most urgent priorities and sharpen the focus of the WSSD.

The Principle of Subsidiarity

7. The WSSD process must ensure that States have the primary responsibility for their own sustainable development with respect to the *principle of subsidiarity*.[11] As cases of assistance become more necessary, as much

---

[8] Cf. Pope John Paul II, *Address to the Pontifical Academy for Social Sciences*, 11 April 2002, No. 3-4.

[9] *Message of Pope John Paul II for the 2000 World Day of Peace*, No. 17.

[10] Pope John Paul II, *Centesimus Annus*, 58.

[11] " Just as it is wrong to withdraw from the individual and commit to the community at large what private enterprise and industry can accomplish, so too it is an injustice, a grave

145

respect as possible for the rightful autonomy and capacity for the self-determination of the person or community being assisted ought to be preserved. Should a State be incapable of meeting its development needs, others are obliged to come to its assistance. This principle applies especially to the efforts towards international sustainable development governance mentioned above, and is vitally important for the preservation of cultural identity.

The calls of the WSSD to promote *good governance* are significant, especially with regard to fighting corruption, promoting more participatory systems, establishing well-functioning bureaucracies and regulatory systems, enforcing laws, and protecting human rights. Certainly States can do more to enrich the notion of political community and encourage the active and responsible involvement of persons in public affairs and decision-making. These efforts can indeed greatly improve the chances for sustainable development.

Future Challenges

8. In terms of material progress, the WSSD has the opportunity to increase the gains already made in the last 10 years. There have been nearly universal improvements in areas such as life expectancy at birth, infant mortality and under-5 mortality rates, nourishment, literacy, school enrolment, income, gender equality, environmental sustainability and democracy. Even more promising are recent findings that technology can be a leading engine, and not only a result, of human development. Building on this progress is surely a form of sustainable development, as future generations will inherit superior living standards. A main priority should be to include least developed countries in the expanding circle of productivity and exchange. While there are many complex reasons why these countries have not progressed at the same rate of other developing countries, there are a number of steps that could be taken to improve their situation.

evil and a disturbance of right order for a larger and higher organization to arrogate to itself functions which can be performed efficiently by smaller and lower bodies" (Pope Pius XI, *Quadragesimo Anno*, 185).

8. *a*) Following the Doha Ministerial meeting, a new round of multilateral trade negotiations aimed at promoting development has been launched. The main focus is to lower trade barriers, especially those that keep the goods and services of developing countries out of developed markets but these barriers also affect trade between developing countries. International agreements must be respected and implemented; at the same time, labor and environmental concerns should not be used as protectionist measures by the developed countries. Rather, developing countries should be encouraged to implement stronger environmental regulations as their incomes rise and in line with their national circumstances.

8. *b*) Developing countries must take steps to provide a better governing infrastructure for sustainable development. The lack of stable institutions and sound policies is often a cause of poverty, one that even increased levels of development assistance cannot overcome. Corruption must be considered a scandal and a major impediment to development. Other aspects of good governance, such as the delivery of adequate education and health services, and the availability of social services that provide temporary relief and re-training for displaced workers, are also necessary. Given the persistent levels of rural poverty in developing countries, rural development cannot be neglected.

8. *c*) Development assistance should be increased and better managed. Although it is just one aspect of international development financing, Official Development Assistance (ODA) is declining. The recommendations of the Monterrey Conference to enhance the coherence and consistency of international monetary, financial and trading systems in support of development are notable. Private capital flows and foreign direct investment should also be encouraged, with respect to the recipient countries' long-term needs.

These three widely-recognized steps – lowering trade barriers, improving the governing infrastructure, and increasing development assistance – should be reinforced at the WSSD, and as far as possible, implemented with a renewed sense of moral purpose and urgency.

The Gift of Self

9. Human dignity is based on the uniqueness of the human being from the rest of creation; that of being made in the image and likeness of God. This however does not entitle the person to be selfish. "This likeness shows that man, the only creature on earth that God wanted for its own sake, cannot fully find himself except in sincere self-giving ".[12] The gift of self ultimately ensures the well-being of others and of future generations.

The human person is created free precisely in order to be able to give himself to others. This self-giving forms the basis of marriage and family life, the first communion of persons through which we all enter the world. This is also the basis of other types of voluntary associations and partnerships which the WSSD wishes to promote. In fact, it is no exaggeration to say that every sign of corruption and abuse in the world is a result of *selfishness and pride*, the very opposites of self-giving.[13]

In the context of sustainability, it must be recalled that members of future generations depend on the gift of self as well, for they rely on the present generation to exercise self-mastery and responsibility. Young people especially rely on the generous sacrifices of others in their education. In a most basic way, self-restraint and dedication to others are bound together, and even seemingly small forms of human love and charity can indeed have great social consequences.[14] In a fundamental and often overlooked way, the *gift of self* is the noblest use of human freedom and the basis for all actions toward integral human development.

---

[12] Second Vatican Council, *Gaudium et Spes*, 24.
[13] *Ibid.* No. 25.
[14] Pope John Paul II, *Evangelium Vitae*, 86.

Appendix Two

Common Declaration of Pope John Paul II and the Ecumenical Patriarch Bartholomew I
Rome – Venice, 10 June 2002

We are gathered here today in the spirit of peace for the good of all human beings and for the care of creation. At this moment in history, at the beginning of the third millennium, we are saddened to see the daily suffering of a great number of people from violence, starvation, poverty and disease. We are also concerned about the negative consequences for humanity and for all creation resulting from the degradation of some basic natural resources such as water, air and land, brought about by an economic and technological progress which does not recognize and take into account its limits.

Almighty God envisioned a world of beauty and harmony, and He created it, making every part an expression of His freedom, wisdom and love (cf. *Gn* 1: 1-25).

At the centre of the whole of creation, He placed us, human beings, with our inalienable human dignity. Although we share many features with the rest of the living beings, Almighty God went further with us and gave us an immortal soul, the source of self-awareness and freedom, endowments that make us in His image and likeness (cf. *Gn* 1: 26-31; 2: 7). Marked with that resemblance, we have been placed by God in the world in order to cooperate with Him in realizing more and more fully the divine purpose for creation.

At the beginning of history, man and woman sinned by disobeying God and rejecting His design for creation. Among the results of this first sin was the destruction of the original harmony of creation. If we examine carefully the social and environmental crisis which the world community is facing, we must conclude that we are still betraying the mandate God has given us: to be stewards called to collaborate with God in watching over creation in holiness and wisdom.

God has not abandoned the world. It is His will that His design and our hope for it will be realized through our co-operation in restoring its original harmony. In our own time we are witnessing a growth of an *ecological awareness* which needs to be encouraged, so that it will lead to practical programmes and initiatives. An awareness of the relationship between God and humankind brings a fuller sense of the importance of the relationship between human beings and the natural environment, which is God's creation and which God entrusted to us to guard with wisdom and love (cf. *Gn* 1: 28).

Respect for creation stems from respect for human life and dignity. It is on the basis of our recognition that the world is created by God that we can discern an objective moral order within which to articulate a code of environmental ethics. In this perspective, Christians and all other believers have a specific role to play in proclaiming moral values and in educating people in *ecological awareness*, which is none other than responsibility towards self, towards others, towards creation.

What is required is an act of repentance on our part and a renewed attempt to view ourselves, one another, and the world around us within the perspective of the divine design for creation. The problem is not simply economic and technological; it is moral and spiritual. A solution at the economic and technological level can be found only if we undergo, in the most radical way, an inner change of heart, which can lead to a change in lifestyle and of unsustainable patterns of consumption and production. A genuine *conversion* in Christ will enable us to change the way we think and act.

First, we must regain humility and recognize the limits of our powers, and most importantly, the limits of our knowledge and judgement. We have been making decisions, taking actions and assigning values that are leading us away from the world as it should be, away from the design of God for creation, away from all that is essential for a healthy planet and a healthy commonwealth of people. A new approach and a new culture are needed, based on the centrality of the human person within creation and inspired by environmentally ethical behavior stemming from our triple relationship to God, to self and to creation. Such an ethics fosters interdependence and stresses the principles of universal solidarity, social justice and responsibility, in order to promote a true culture of life.

Secondly, we must frankly admit that humankind is entitled to something better than what we see around us. We and, much more, our children and future generations are entitled to a better world, a world free from degradation, violence and bloodshed, a world of generosity and love.

Thirdly, aware of the value of prayer, we must implore God the Creator to enlighten people everywhere regarding the duty to respect and carefully guard creation.

We therefore invite all men and women of good will to ponder the importance of the following ethical goals:

1. To think of the world's children when we reflect on and evaluate our options for action.

2. To be open to study the true values based on the natural law that sustain every human culture.

3. To use science and technology in a full and constructive way, while recognizing that the findings of science have always to be evaluated in the light of the centrality of the human person, of the common good and of the inner purpose of creation. Science may help us to correct the mistakes of the past, in order to enhance the spiritual and material well-being of the present and future generations. It is love for our children that will show us the path that we must follow into the future.

4. To be humble regarding the idea of ownership and to be open to the demands of solidarity. Our mortality and our weakness of judgement together warn us not to take irreversible actions with what we choose to regard as our property during our brief stay on this earth. We have not been entrusted with unlimited power over creation, we are only stewards of the common heritage.

5. To acknowledge the diversity of situations and responsibilities in the work for a better world environment. We do not expect every person and every institution to assume the same burden. Everyone has a part to play, but for the demands of justice and charity to be respected the most affluent societies must carry the greater burden, and from them is demanded a sacrifice greater than can be offered by the poor. Religions, governments and institutions are faced by many different situations; but on the basis of the principle of subsidiarity all of them can take on some tasks, some part of the shared effort.

6. To promote a peaceful approach to disagreement about how to live on this earth, about how to share it and use it, about what to change and what to leave unchanged. It is not our desire to evade controversy about the environment, for we trust in the capacity of human reason and the path of dialogue to reach agreement. We commit ourselves to respect the views of all who disagree with us, seeking solutions through open exchange, without resorting to oppression and domination.

It is not too late. God's world has incredible healing powers. Within a single generation, we could steer the earth toward our children's future. Let that generation start now, with God's help and blessing.